The Charm Bracelet
and Other Stories

Anne Hall Norris

Creekwood Press

Library of Congress Control Number: 2001090783

ISBN 0-9652829-4-5

Published by: CREEKWOOD PRESS
                Memphis, Tennessee
                2001

Cover design by Joanna Harris

Printed in the United States of America

The Charm Bracelet
and Other Stories

*Dedicated to
my husband Felix Norris
and to my children,
Gary Wagoner, Michael Wagoner
and Janet Harris*

IN APPRECIATION

To my son Gary Wagoner for his story illustrations. To my granddaughter Joanna Harris for cover design. To Madge Lewis, Ruth Crenshaw and Ann Huckaba, members of the Memphis Story Tellers' League, for their support and encouragement. To publisher Jim Gray for his guidance and patience.

Contents

Contents

The Charm Bracelet
and Other Stories

THE CHARM BRACELET

My heart was pounding as I reached for the phone. I glanced at the clock on my bedside table. Not even 5:30—still dark outside. No one would be calling this early in the morning unless there was an emergency.

"Granny, Granny, wake up!" It was Joanna, my oldest granddaughter, and she was fairly shouting with excitement.

"What's wrong?" I stammered. "Has there been an accident?" I knew something terrible must have happened.

"No, Granny, It's your silver charm bracelet. It's been found. I know it's your bracelet."

Joanna was making no sense at all. I had lost my bracelet ten years earlier while on a trip to London. Broken hearted over the loss, I had extended my trip an extra week in the hope that my offer of a substantial reward would result in the return of the bracelet. Finally convinced that the sterling mementos of so many special times and events in my life were gone forever, I had returned to my home in Memphis.

"It's in the morning paper, Granny," Joanna said. "I *know* it's yours. There's a picture of the bracelet and the double-frame charm, with the pictures of your mother and daddy, and there's one with the name of your school and a graduation date." She was hardly pausing for a breath. "The man who has it is trying to find the owner, Granny. You've got to call him and tell him it's yours!"

"Slow down, Honey," I said. "I don't know what you are talking about, and my paper hasn't been delivered yet."

"Well, I'm on my way over with mine, Granny. I'll see you in twenty minutes."

Putting on my robe and slippers, I told myself this had to be some kind of mistake. How could someone have found my bracelet and now have it back in Memphis? I would not get my hopes up, but the possibility was definitely exciting!

The bracelets were very popular when I was a teenager and mine, with a "Sweet 16" charm, was a birthday present from my parents. The following Christmas they had added the charm that Joanna said was pictured in the paper. It was a double frame holding pictures of my mother and father. Over the years other charms were added to commemorate milestones in my life—scholastic awards, vacations, high school sweethearts, my wedding day, births of my children and grandchildren. There was a story behind each one.

The little key was a gift from the boy next door who was my first real date. We were "steadies" for almost two years. "The key to my heart," he had said when I opened his present that Valentine's Day. His family moved to Chicago the following year. We corresponded for a few months and there were phone calls at first, but young hearts have a way of mending fast. Years later I heard he had married a girl he met in college and they were living in upstate New York.

When my daughter left for college, she added the silver telephone to my bracelet. "So you won't forget to call me occasionally," she said as we hugged goodbye. I missed her so much there was no chance of my forgetting!

I especially liked the little convertible, a souvenir from a trip to Palm Springs for a business conference, after which a friend and I rented the open top car and drove along the coast of California. For an entire week we explored the little shops in Carmel and Monterey, ate wonderful seafood at Fisherman's Wharf, saw beautiful sunsets over the ocean and then at night, under the stars, we strolled along the beaches.

Waiting for Joanna to come with the paper, I thought of the many other charms the bracelet held—the one my older son had given me when he received the Boy Scout's "God and Country" Award. He was only fourteen at the time. He added the Eagle Scout charm the following year.

The heart-shaped charm was from Michael—a Mother's Day present the year he moved to Florida. "Special Mom" was engraved on the front, with his name and the date on the back.

When I made my first solo flight, my long–time friend Esther sent me the tiny airplane engraved with the date of the accomplishment. She added another charm a few months later when I earned my pilot's license and joined the Ninety–Nines, Inc., the organization of women pilots founded by Amelia Earhart. My participation with Esther several years in the Powder Puff Derby, the all–woman transcontinental air race, resulted in a number of mementos, almost filling my bracelet.

The last charm I added was the funny looking cat with green eyes—appropriately from my daughter. Janet has loved cats all her life. It is strange how many cats just "followed her home" when she was in school. She has two house cats now, along with two dogs, two birds, a hamster, and a turtle. She also has two aquariums and an outdoor pool with goldfish.

I was lost in my reminiscing when the doorbell rang. Joanna thrust the paper into my hand and pointed to the picture. There was no mistake. I didn't have to read the accompanying article, which gave a name and phone number to call. The pictures of my mother and father removed any doubt I might have had.

To say I was curious as to where my bracelet had been found and how it had made its way back to Memphis would be an understatement. I was pacing the floor like an expectant father, but knew I couldn't make the phone call at such a ghastly hour on a Saturday morning.

"Not before eight o'clock," I told Joanna. "A lot of folks like to sleep late on weekends."

Finally the grandfather clock chimed eight times. I was almost too nervous to dial the phone and ready to offer an apology for the early morning call. No need. A very pleasant voice bade me, "Good Morning and God's blessing. This is John speaking."

"John," I said, "this is the old lady who lost the bracelet."

Wanting to verify that I was the rightful owner, he asked the school I had attended and my graduation date and several other bits of information that only I would have known.

"Lady," he said, "I have your bracelet and you may come and get it any time."

I almost went into shock when he gave me his address—only two blocks from my home! Needless to say, Joanna and I were on our way within the next five minutes!

John greeted us with a big smile, opening his left hand to reveal the bracelet looped over his thumb. My knees were weak as I threw my arms around him and softly wept, too overwhelmed to speak for a few moments. I wanted to hear the whole story of how it had come into his possession.

Biking through England during summer vacation, John's nephew and several of his college friends had stopped at a pawn shop, curious as to what kinds of merchandise they might find in the small establishment several miles north of London. Examining the bracelet, the young man had noticed a charm that was the replica of the identifying on–site sign of an international hotel chain headquartered in Memphis. He remembered hearing his Uncle John tell about the opening of the system's first hotel and his long–time friendship with the founder, Kemmons Wilson.

According to the shop owner, the bracelet had been pawned several years earlier. He recalled that a middle–aged woman brought it in, claiming to be temporarily short of cash. She had never returned to redeem it nor had anyone until now shown interest in making the purchase.

John's nephew, always intrigued by mysteries, felt there might be some connection between the bracelet and the hotel chain. He sent it to his uncle with a note advising that the bracelet should be given to the owner with his compliments should she ever be found; thus my offer of a reward was flatly refused.

"But tell me," John said, "for my nephew will want to know. Is there a connection between you and the Holiday Inn hotel system?"

"A connection that spanned over a period of 32 years," I said, explaining that the 'Great Sign' charm had been a service award on the anniversary of my 25th year with the company. Just as that sign directed travelers for nearly half a century, its tiny replica led to the return of my bracelet.

As we drove away with the bracelet dangling from my wrist, I waved and called, "Thank you, John, and thanks to your nephew." Then I whispered. "And thank you, Kemmons Wilson!"

TO CALIFORNIA IN A BOX

No one except my brother–in–law Egbert would have even considered such an adventure. It was 1946, World War II was history, and gas was no longer rationed. Egbert had completed an overhaul job on his old Chrysler sedan and was certain the drive from Memphis to Los Angeles would be a snap.

My brother–in–law was not a detail man, but he could come up with some mind–boggling ideas, and this one was a prize–winner. The trip would be educational and so much fun, it should be enjoyed by more than just him and my sister and their three daughters, ages five, nine and eleven. At Egbert's invitation and insistence, my brother Adam, his wife and two young children were added to the passenger list. To even out the number, he invited me, a sixteen–year–old who had never been outside of Shelby County.

Always the optimist, Egbert was sure ten of us in one car would be no problem. He drew plans and set about to build a box for the trunk. "The box" extended about two feet beyond the trunk of the car. It had high sideboards and a like-size board across the protruding end. In case of a sudden stop, this hopefully would prevent whatever, or whoever, was in "the box" from landing on the highway. It should be noted that the network of interstate highways stretching across our nation today had not then been constructed.

Had my mother been living at that time, it is unlikely I would have been participating in this marvelous, educational trip. That is because my "box seat" likely would have been occupied by Mama, who was always ready for a new adventure. It was not too difficult to convince my 75–year–old father that this would be the opportunity of my life. I would be under the watchful care of an older brother and sister. What could go wrong?

I am not sure whether air–conditioners for cars had been invented back then. I only know that my brother–in–law's car didn't have one. What we had was a canvas bag that was filled with water and fastened onto the front of the car over the radiator. I think this somehow cooled the engine. It did nothing to cool the passengers.

Most of the time, two of my nieces and I rode in "the box." This was a lot better than being inside the car with four adults and three other children, which was necessary when we crossed the desert because the heat in the box was unbearable. When we rode in the box we would watch for oncoming cars and wave at those who peered at us in total disbelief. This did not meet with the approval of my brother-in-law, especially when cars got so close he feared for our safety should he have to make a sudden stop. The girls and I enjoyed the attention and could not understand how our waving and shouting could in any way create potentially dangerous travel conditions.

As might be surmised, with ten people in the car (one way or another) there was little room for anything else. The necessities, therefore, rode on top. This included assorted pieces of luggage (using the term broadly) and our camping equipment. It would be an understatement to say that we were on a limited budget. Egbert had figured exactly how many miles we would travel and how much gas would be needed. He did not anticipate any emergencies, but stressed that we could not afford to be extravagant in our spending.

Most nights we camped "out." That is "out" as *out in the middle of the desert.* My sister–in–law was scared of the little varmints that scamper about in the dark, so she opted for the back seat of the car. The littlest ones were bedded down on the front seat. The luckiest ones got the box, and the rest shared quilts spread on the ground. My sister usually made the morning campfire, sometimes from dried cacti, and the aroma of perking coffee would get the rest of us up and ready for another adventurous day.

We never stayed in any of those wonderful RV parks that are along the major highways today. Even had they been available back then, it is doubtful our RV would have been welcome. We did, however, stay in a motel about every third night. This was absolutely essential so that we all could take baths and laundering could be done. Due to limited space, we were permitted to take very few changes of clothing.

One of the places on our "must see" list was the Painted Desert. I remember it well. We were a little behind schedule that day because we had encountered a terrible desert sandstorm. The highway suddenly disappeared under a blanket of swirling sand. With zero visibility, we had to sit in the car and wait out the storm. This was a most memorable experience. A hot July day in the middle of a desert. Four tired adults, five irritable children and one disillusioned teenager, all inside one car with the windows closed and no air conditioning. Not an adventure to be soon forgotten.

The storm having caused us to get off of our schedule, the sign pointing out the Painted Desert was almost a blur. "There it is, off to the right. Everybody get a good look!" shouted Egbert as we sped on our way. We did, however, enjoy the wonders of Carlsbad Caverns. The price of admission evidently had been figured into our budget because we took one of the guided tours.

We spent two nights at Grand Canyon National Park, arriving there late one afternoon. The mule train which daily takes tourists down to the river at the bottom of the canyon and back, was sold out for the following day. No problem. The round–trip was only 14 miles. Egbert, Adam, my sister and I could easily walk that far if we got an early start. My sister-in-law volunteered to stay with the children. In retrospect, I can see that she made a lot of wise decisions.

At the crack of dawn, the four of us were ready to hit the trail. Not wanting to carry any unnecessary items, we each had a small water bottle and several lemons in our pockets. Although the temperature rose to around 100 degrees and the sand on the trail was several inches deep, going down wasn't too bad. We moved aside and waved as the mule train passed us going down. Later in the day we again moved aside and waved as the mule train passed us once more, on its way back up. We were still on the way down.

Giving us words of encouragement, some of the riders said they had left snacks for us at the rest area. What a treat when we finally got there! We cooled our feet in the clear water of the canyon river, rested awhile, and started the long, uphill trek back. The day that had begun so wonderfully now was ending with us still several miles below the park lodge where we had left my sister–in–law and the five children.

My sister's pace had slowed, but she walked on without complaining. I would walk a few steps and stop, certain I could go no farther. I was thirsty, hungry and tired. Egbert threatened me with tales of wild canyon animals that came out after dark and killed everyone they encountered. I was too tired to care. As darkness began to settle in, Adam decided to leave us and get back to the lodge as quickly as possible to let the park rangers know that we were still on the trail.

We saw nothing on the entire trip more wonderful than the sight of four park rangers coming down to meet us. Helped along by two of them, I managed to make the last mile. It was after we were back in the lodge that we learned it was a rarity for anyone to make the 14–mile trip on foot during the summer months.

Eventually we did reach the West Coast. Two days later we were headed back home. Our trip was a great success. Not only had we seen some of nature's most outstanding attractions, we had enjoyed the hospitality of California relatives, made lifelong friends along the way, and proved that ten people in one car can endure a 5,000–mile trip—provided they are adventurous, not claustrophobic, and don't mind traveling in a box.

THE APOSTROPHE

That pesky little apostrophe
Is something that bugs me.
I see it almost every day
Where it shouldn't ought to be.
The new store has "it's" opening;
The lion has "it's" mighty roar,
And according to their mailbox,
"The Smith's" have moved next door.

THE RED BRICK HOUSE

Sitting under the magnolia tree, I watched as the operator of the giant yellow bulldozer steered the powerful machine toward the red brick house. My children had said I shouldn't come—that it would be too painful, but I felt compelled to witness the demolition.

When their father and I married nearly a half-century earlier, the 29-foot house trailer we bought wouldn't hold a candle to today's spacious models. Ours was not a "park model" such as my younger son now owns. It was just a plain house trailer, although it didn't do any "trailing" except for the three times it was moved. Each time after it was parked, the wheels were removed and the trailer was set upon some railroad cross ties. For four years there were just the two of us, and our trailer was like a cozy dollhouse, divided into three areas—living area, kitchen area, and bed area. It would be an exaggeration to refer to those areas as rooms, although there was a sliding door between the kitchen area and bed area. In addition to the bed, dresser/chest and tiny closet, the bed area also had a stall shower. Further bathroom facilities were reached via a path across the back yard.

Our first baby's arrival presented some challenges. When he outgrew the laundry basket, his crib had to be squeezed in between the couch and the dining table. Still I was satisfied with our trailer house—most of the time. It was the pending arrival of our second baby that caused me concern. As I explained to my husband, "We don't even have room for the laundry basket now, much less another crib." However minor problems, such as where to put another baby, never seemed to bother their father. He was sure I could handle everything, and he was right. I soon found a half-acre lot for sale not far from where our trailer was parked. At the back of the property there was a small building where the owners spent weekends away from their city home. Although sparsely furnished, there was a bed, sofa, table with two chairs, stove, and a few cabinets. Water from the deep well was piped into the kitchen sink—no hot water, of course. And there was a path leading to the far corner of the lot, where the little house with the half-moon cutout on the door was located.

The owners of the property, after spending a few weekends there, had decided country living was not for them. They were pleased to find buyers and accepted the small down payment, which wiped out our meager savings account. We worked out a plan to pay off the balance in monthly notes over the next several years.

Wheels were put back onto the trailer and it was pulled to the newly acquired property and parked next to the existing building. The trailer door and the door to the building were aligned, so that we could easily step from one structure to the other, although they were a couple of feet apart. We all still slept in the trailer, but the children liked to play in the "annex" because there was room to spread out their toys. It also was better than the trailer for entertaining visitors. The situation wasn't ideal, but it definitely was an improvement. In fact, things were going rather smoothly until I saw the magazine article. The headlines caught my attention: "Complete House Plans with List of All Materials Required: $10." My check was in the mail the next day.

I waited until the plans came before mentioning this do–it–yourself project to my husband. I was sure he would say it was a stupid idea. I was right. That was exactly what he said because the only building he had ever done was the construction of the little house at the end of the path where our trailer was previously located. Even that didn't turn out exactly as he had planned. He had to make several trips to the lumberyard as the size of the building increased, eventually becoming big enough for a storage shed at one end. "We don't know anything about building a house," he argued.

"Don't worry," I said, "I will handle everything."

With the two boys in tow, I visited a neighbor who I had heard some folks refer to as a "jackleg carpenter." I wasn't sure exactly what that meant, but I later came to believe it had something to do with the way he did his measuring. I noticed he would lay out his tape measure, look at it carefully, and then say "That's approximately about…" Nevertheless, he agreed to dig the footing and put up the framework at an hourly rate that sounded good to me. The boys and I made the rounds of local lumberyards, finding the best prices, and ordering the materials specified in the plans while "Mr. Cap" (the name the children gave to our "approximately about" carpenter) dug the trenches and set up forms for the footings. At that time my husband was employed by a ready-mix cement company. We decided it would be more practical to pour solid concrete footings than to use the concrete blocks specified in the plans. There was one big problem. Mr. Cap's forms split apart when the first load of cement was poured into them. That was only the first of many trials and tribulations, as I continued to assure my husband that everything was under control.

About six months after the ground breaking, our house was framed up, with windows in place and shingles on the roof. Black saturated felt covered the outside walls; however a problem arose before the brick work could be done.

We were out of money!

A wonderful gentleman who had passed our house several times a week, watching our progress, noticed that work seemingly had ceased. His loan made it possible for work to continue.

Fortunately my husband was able to do all the plumbing and electrical work. Together we put up ceiling tile and installed sheet rock on the walls. It had become a family project and even our older son helped sand the seams. Mr. Cap helped us locate a bricklayer. His work looked good, but he needed a small cash advance. It wasn't until we gave him his second, and larger, advance that he disappeared—never to return! Somehow we managed to find a bricklayer to finish the job.

The do–it–yourself instructions gave us building plans, but not the information we needed for doing work on the inside. We learned that a sealer must be put onto hardwood floors before the varnish or the wood turns black. It is then necessary to rent a sander and use lots and lots of sandpaper to repair the damage. We also learned it is not wise to spread glue over the entire area where vinyl floor covering is to be installed. Walking on the glued surface to place the vinyl all the way into the corner is a sticky mess!

Ten months from the start of construction we were settled into our house. When we moved eleven years later to be near the school our children were attending, we rented the house to a young pilot and his wife. Five years later they were able to buy a house of their own, and in less than a week a family of four became our new renters. Following their departure, we made the property available to a Cambodian refugee family. Their "temporary stay" lasted three years. They were barely out of the house when our older son finished college and moved in, joined several years later by his bride. When they purchased their own house, our younger son took up residence in his childhood home and remained there until he moved to Florida and we sold the property.

The big yellow machine slowly moved forward and a minute later dust rose from the pile of rubble that once had been a red brick house. I wiped a tear from my eye and then I thanked God for all who had been blessed by the "do–it–yourself house," built by determination, hard work, and an abundant supply of love.

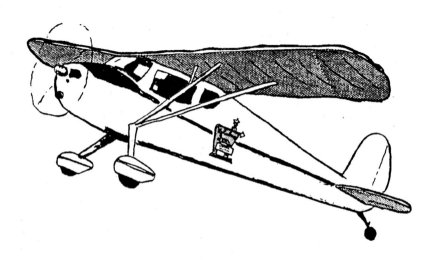

THE POWDER PUFF DERBY

It took two years for me to get smart enough to realize the extent of my stupidity. I was lying on my back, waxing the belly of the small single–engine airplane when this realization came to me like a bolt of lightning. I'm not sure what brought this on—whether the 90–degree temperature, the rough concrete pavement, the sweat bees circling my face, or all of the above. As I lay there, however, I contemplated the many hours I had spent waxing and polishing, removing bugs from the windshield, making certain the plane was properly refueled, and handling other such mundane chores.

Meanwhile Esther and Betty, the proficient pilots of this wondrous machine, were in the air–conditioned office of the mayor, receiving keys to the city, being interviewed by a local newspaper reporter, or preparing for a television appearance.

Esther, the plane's owner and chief pilot, was a vivacious lady from south Georgia. She was a franchise holder with a multi–million dollar company and served as the only female member of its international advisory board. This, coupled with her abundance of charm, led to her obtaining the company's sponsorship in the Powder Puff Derby, an all–woman transcontinental air race. As a public relations employee of the sponsoring company, I had been assigned to handle the team's publicity, which involved accompanying Esther and Betty on a pre–race inspections flight to the West Coast where the race would begin.

As I became less enchanted with my assignment and the associated duties—which were both mentally and physically exhausting—I reasoned that if I were a licensed pilot, I could bump Betty from the co–pilot's seat and enjoy some of the celebrity treatment the team received. I envisioned myself as becoming a member of the famed Ninety-Nines, Inc., the organization of licensed women pilots founded by Amelia Earhart. I thought how proud this would have made my father, who was keenly interested in every aspect of flying. He was a contemporary of the Wright Brothers, being only three years younger than Orville Wright, and a great admirer of these aviation pioneers.

I recalled how Papa would load all of us into the old truck on Sunday afternoons when I was a child and head for the airport. He would find a shady place to park and we would spend hours watching the airplanes, which today would seem like mere toys. No jumbo jets back then—just small propeller–type planes, usually painted yellow or red. Papa would get excited when one lifted from the ground. He marveled over the wonder of these flying machines and dreamed of the day he himself might have an opportunity to go up in an airplane and soar over the countryside. His dream was never fulfilled.

Mama didn't share Papa's enthusiasm. In fact, she wasn't sure airplanes were here to stay. Mama often said if man were meant to fly, God would have given him wings. I figured the same went for women and children, although I never actually heard her say that. I took it for granted that Mama was right, especially after my oldest brother—always the studious one in our family—made a pair of wings for me. After securing the plywood wings to my outstretched arms, he hurled me into the air from the top of our barn to see if I would be able to fly. I couldn't.

While I never shared Mama's conviction that flying was for the birds, neither did I have Papa's enthusiasm for airplanes. I never had considered becoming a pilot, certainly not participating in a cross–country air race. Nevertheless, three weeks after I experienced the amazing revelation regarding my stupidity, I began studying for a pilot's license.

I had no idea how much one must learn before actually operating a plane. Ground school comes first. That's where all the rules for navigating are taught. It's a different world up there in the sky where there are no highways or road signs to follow.

I was fortunate to have a wonderful flight instructor, a handsome commercial pilot who gave private lessons when his schedule permitted. Still there were times when I almost gave up, like the day I was struggling with a particular maneuver and my instructor assured me he could teach a chimp to fly! I told him to go find a chimp because I had decided I was no longer interested in becoming a pilot. Fortunately for me, he said he didn't hear what I said, nor did he want it repeated.

Five months after I received my pilot's license, preparations were underway for the annual derby. Since Betty had no connection with the sponsor, I booted her out of the right–hand seat as planned and signed up for the race from California to New Jersey. Esther and I wore matching outfits in bright yellow and green, the colors of our sponsor. Her plane had been painted in the same colors, with the company's emblem on the doors. We looked good!

The flight from Memphis to San Diego, where all planes would be impounded for a week while being checked by Federal Aviation inspectors, was as exciting as the race itself. Following the race route, we not only generated publicity for our sponsor, but also were able to familiarize ourselves with the airports that would be required stops or fly–over check points during the race. All went well until we were headed down the runway at one of the airports and a flock of seagulls flew up directly in front of the plane. Although the propeller hit one of them, we made a safe departure.

Later that day our engine failed just after we had gotten airborne. As Esther struggled to regain power, I declared an emergency and we were cleared for immediate landing. After the mechanics ruled our plane safe to fly, we were off for our next adventure. This came as we were crossing the Rocky Mountains and the generator belt broke. Turning off all auxiliary equipment, we maintained enough power for the operation of one radio and once again made a safe landing.

The actual race, with a hundred teams competing, was not so much for monetary awards as for the glory of winning. Although nothing could be done to alter the plane itself in any way, including mechanical changes or removal of factory furnishings, fixtures or equipment, the ladies made personal efforts to lighten the weight and thereby increase speed potential. Some went on diets for months and limited their carry–on bags to little more than tooth brush and change of underwear.

One team began the race wearing disposable dresses made from a paper product manufactured by their sponsoring company. Their dresses were disposed of sooner than planned, however, as they had closed the air vents to prevent unnecessary drag and make for better speed. It was so hot inside the plane, the dresses disintegrated. The embarrassed ladies deplaned wrapped in the air map/charts they were using during the race.

A team of Canadians, flying with closed air vents, stripped to their undergarments, not considering that when they flew low over a check point, there would be spectators with binoculars.

The Powder Puff Derby grew to become the largest air race in the world, with participants from Europe, Asia, Australia, New Zealand, and many other countries. It was discontinued after a discrimination charge was filed by male pilots who wanted to be included.

The years I participated in the race did not bring me blue ribbons or trophies, but the satisfaction of having "been there, done that." The challenges that were met and the experiences gained may be relived through the pages of a scrapbook, which I titled "Powder Puff Derby—My Tribute to Papa."

THE ADVENTURE
OF TWO STORYTELLERS

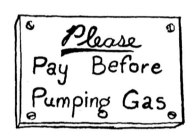

This is a story of Joycie and Anne,
Who set out one night with a definite plan.
They were off to Mississippi, this awesome pair,
For they had some wonderful stories to share.
The invitation came from a ladies' church group.
"Come early for sandwiches and maybe some soup."
Neither was familiar with the roads they would take,
But they'd started out early, for goodness sake!
The evening was dark, and rainy, and cold.
Not to bother...these gals were ever so bold.
Joycie was driving her new automobile,
No trouble at all with her at the wheel!
She stopped by for Anne with time to spare;
And off they went, that jovial pair.
The traffic was heavy—quite enough to scare;
The road signs all read: "Slow. Under Repair."
But Joycie and Anne were quite content.
They talked and laughed a lot as they went.

They agreed on stories they'd tell that night.
They both felt confident all would go right.
The four-lane highway soon gave way to two.
The cars they met now were only a few.
No street lights to guide them as they went along.
No bother to them...What could go wrong!
Joycie had directions, or so she thought;
For emergency, a cell phone they'd brought.
As they traveled along in conversation deep,
From somewhere unknown came a loud beep.
And Joycie, driving the car that was new,
Wondered aloud what was it that blew.
The panel didn't show any emergency light.
The oil wasn't low and the brakes were tight.
Then Joycie remembered what she ought to have done,
For without gas in the tank, a car just won't run
The fuel gauge sank to the near–empty spot,
And Joycie lamented she had somehow forgot.
"No worry," she said, "we can still go for miles."
Her voice was confident; her face was all smiles.
Now Anne wasn't so sure that Joycie was right.
But just up ahead, there was a station in sight.
"Maybe we should get some gas," Joycie said,
"Now that the fuel gauge is down in the red."
She drove to the pump and quickly jumped out.
She opened the tank and put in the spout.
The gas pump was on. Oh, what a surprise!
No "pay in advance" as one might surmise.
For the hour was late and the station was small.
Some pump gas and leave, not paying at all.
These Mississippi folks, how trustful they are,
Thought Anne as she waited inside the car.
Then out from the station there came a young man.
He walked up to Joycie, his cap in his hand.
"You can pump 'til twelve dollars," he said with a grin.

But Joycie advised she had planned to spend ten.
"Whatever you please," the young man replied.
"But I paid twelve dollars when I went inside."
Then Joycie realized what she had done;
Someone had paid, but she wasn't the one.
This was an advance–pay station, you see,
And Joycie was pumping her gas for free!
The man who parked opposite had gone in to pay.
She was using his money, to his utter dismay!
But she gave him a smile and said she didn't know;
She'd just started the pump 'cause her gas was so low.
Joycie used the twelve dollars and then
Paid in full—though she'd planned to spend ten!
They drove away laughing because they knew well
They had given this man a wild story to tell.
They soon found the church; they weren't even late.
The ladies were cordial and the meal was just great.
Now these two storytellers were a tremendous hit.
They performed professionally, not stumbling a bit
But Joycie and Anne were really quite smitten
When one of the ladies told a story she'd written.
She's better than us, the two readily agreed.
It's folks like her we need in our League.
An invitation they gave before taking their leave,
And what happened next is hard to believe.
The lady in charge had a few words to say
Before Joycie and Anne could get on their way.
She thanked them profusely for the stories they told,
For venturing out on a night wet and cold.
She said, "What a blessing to us you have been;
We hope you'll come back and visit again.
We know you don't charge, but you've traveled so far.
Please accept this ten dollars and gas up your car!"

CASA NORRIS

That's the sign over the workbench in our garage, where my husband Felix makes customized golf clubs. It's a memento of an adventure in Acapulco that we aren't likely to forget.

Working with the board of directors of an international hotel organization offered many advantages, one being that we were privileged to attend meetings with association members throughout the world. Host hotels always provided our group with their finest services and facilities. The high–rise hotel in Acapulco was no exception.

Finding our rooms was made easy by the hand–painted signs attached to the doors, identifying them as our *casa* or home while at the hotel. "Home was never like this," I said to Felix as we walked out onto our balcony. The view from the twelfth floor was breathtaking. Directly below was the swimming pool and courtyard, beyond which we could see the ocean and the hotel's private beach.

A reception on the night we arrived began with each guest being given a tiny clay cup on a cord, placed over our head like a necklace. The purpose became clear as we stepped inside the room where the party was held. Greeters at the door filled our thimble-size cups with tequila, the popular Mexican drink. While the food, music, and entertainment were magnificent, Felix and I had one experience definitely not planned by our hosts.

Tired from the long flight, we were among the first to leave the party and retreated to Casa Norris, intent upon enjoying the sights and sounds of the evening from our private balcony for a while before retiring.

Following posted instructions, Felix locked the door with the dead bolt as soon as we entered our room and then added the double security of a secondary device that seemingly would prevent any unwanted intrusion.

Relaxing in lounge chairs on our balcony, we could faintly hear the music from the continuing party, where some of our group likely would dance the night away. The moon was bright, the sky was filled with millions of twinkling stars, and a cool breeze made for a perfect evening. Jet lag overtook me, however, and soon I was nodding. Felix suggested we go inside, knowing I would have an early meeting the next morning.

A look of disbelief was on his face as Felix attempted to open the sliding glass door. "We're locked out," he said, continuing to tug at the handle. I felt sure he must be mistaken since certainly neither of us had put the lock on the door when we walked out onto the balcony.

"That's impossible," I said—but it wasn't. We were locked outside on the balcony of our twelfth floor room.

I saw a few people in the courtyard and yelled to

them as I waved my arms. Not within hearing distance, some waved back.

"I know what I will do," I said to Felix, "I have on a white half-slip. I can take it off and wave it and surely someone will look up and understand that we are in trouble." Always proper and quite reserved, he was horrified at my suggestion.

"Well, don't worry," I said, "we can just sleep out here on these lounge chairs. When I don't show up at the meeting in the morning, someone will come looking for me." He considered that to be an even worse suggestion.

Felix continued tugging at the door although we were in agreement that it definitely was locked. My efforts were as futile as his, but I waved and yelled whenever I spotted a figure below. Some looked up and waved back, evidently unaware of our desperate situation. Finally a couple appeared on a balcony two floors below. "We are locked out of our room," I called. "Please contact the hotel manager."

Ten minutes later as we looked through the sliding door, we could see the knob on the entrance door to our room being turned from the outside. The problem was the secondary lock—a big arm-like device about eight inches long that turned back across the door. As we watched thin blades protrude between the door and the facing, the couple who had summoned our potential rescuers called up encouragement, informing us of all the efforts that were being made to open our door.

As word of the lockout spread, other guests joined in the excitement, filling the corridor outside our room and offering advice. There was a resounding cheer when the door finally was opened. Hurrying across the room, a security officer unlocked the balcony door and a round of applause greeted us as we stepped inside.

"Champagne is on the way," the manager said, "and please accept our apologies for this unfortunate situation."

"No problem," I assured him as I gave Felix a hug. "After all, it's not where you are but who you are with that's important."

When we left the hotel a week later, the Casa Norris sign was given to us.

The experience hasn't discouraged us from occupying upper floor rooms in high–rise hotels; however if we go out onto the balcony, we are very careful to be certain we never, never completely close the door.

WHERE'S
MR. PURDY

J ust the mention of Mr. Purdy sends my friend
Julius and me into fits of laughter.
We've actually never met Mr. Purdy. But he almost
broke up our budding romance.

Julius had come to the city where I live for a business
conference. We had been introduced by a mutual friend
who knew we had a lot of common interests. For one
thing, we were both single parents with teenage children.
The trials and tribulations of parenthood gave us plenty
to talk about during the evening, which included a
wonderful Italian dinner with several bottles of red
wine. We parted at the airport, looking forward to his
return in six weeks.

Julius phoned me at least once a day, and I would
rush home from my office to see what kind of mail I
might have received. Daily cards reflected his great sense
of humor. The florist truck was seen in my driveway so

often, neighbors thought I was having an affair with the delivery man. I think we both had been bitten by the love bug.

My excitement mounted as the day drew near for Julius to return. I had planned to meet him at the airport, and I was a bit apprehensive. After all, it had been six weeks since our one evening together. Would he be as wonderful as I remembered? Maybe I wouldn't recognize him!

The big day finally came. I was up at the crack of dawn. I changed clothes at least six times before settling on what to wear. The new outfit I had bought for the occasion did seem a bit dressy for going to the airport. I decided to save that red silk for the next evening. The blue suit would be more appropriate. Julius liked blue. I was wearing a blue dress when we met, and he said it was a perfect match for my eyes.

This being such a special occasion, I thought I should have my hair done so I made a three o'clock appointment at the beauty shop. Julius' plane wasn't due in until 5:50. I knew I would have plenty of time. Wrong! First off, his plane made a brief stop in Chicago and he dashed off to give me a quick call at the office. The receptionist told him I had gone to the beauty shop. She went on to tell him that I wouldn't be back in the office that afternoon because I was going to meet someone at the airport.

If the manicurist hadn't insisted that I should have my nails done, I wouldn't have been late getting to the airport. I had planned it all so carefully. I would be at the gate waiting. But the plane got there before I did. When I first saw Julius, he was walking down the corridor toward me with an attentive lady at his side. Seeing that they were engaged in conversation, it was obvious to me that they were acquainted. My first thought was that they had been seated next to each other on the plane and would part company when I reached them. Wrong again! When she realized that I was about to extend a welcome to Julius, she actually grabbed his arm. I couldn't believe what I was seeing. I gave Julius a very cool peck on his cheek and waited for an introduction—or an explanation. I got neither.

With Julius in the middle, the three of us walked to the baggage area. Nothing was said until Julius asked me to hold his brief case while he retrieved his bags. That female acquaintance of his (whoever she was!) tried to jerk it right out of my hand. "I will hold that for him," she said. Not on your life, I thought. I yanked it back and told her in no uncertain terms that I would hold the brief case.

Once outside the terminal, I very coolly advised that my car was parked in lane C. "That woman" said emphatically that *her* car was in lane B. Julius just stood there, looking from her to me. "You handle this any way you want to," I said to him, "I'm going to my car." As I opened my car door, I looked back and could see they were still right where I had left them. But I couldn't hear what was being said. Julius turned and headed my way. When he could stop laughing, he explained what had happened.

When he had arrived, he looked for me. Of course I wasn't there since I was late. The mystery lady walked up as if she were expecting him. Right off, he figured she was someone from my office. After all, when he called from Chicago, my overly-efficient receptionist had told him I had gone to the beauty shop. It made sense to him that I had sent one of the secretaries to meet him. He was puzzled, though, when we met in the corridor just a few minutes later and I didn't introduce them. Also, he couldn't understand why he got such a cool reception.

The conversation in the parking lot cleared it up. The lady had been sent to the airport to meet a Mr. Purdy, who was to be the speaker that evening at a convention dinner. Although she had never met Mr. Purdy, the description she had been given fit Julius, and it was obvious he was looking around as though expecting someone to meet him.

One thing had upset the lady. She was shocked that he had a girlfriend, a mistress, or whatever. Even worse, this hussy had the nerve to come to the airport to meet him! Nevertheless, she had been sent to meet Mr. Purdy and take him to the hotel. She intended to do just that.

As Julius and I were putting his bags in my car, we looked back. There she stood, in total disbelief that she had failed her assignment. Tears ran down her cheeks as she wailed, "But where's Mr. Purdy?"

ZAPPED BY AUNT ZEENIE

Her shrill voice pierced the early morning air. As I bounded up the steps of Aunt Zeenie's front porch, I could hear her screaming, "No, No. Don't do that to me again!" My heart was pounding as I flung open the unlocked door and raced through the house, expecting the worst. It wasn't that I had not told her hundreds of times to keep her doors locked. She just could not believe anything bad could happen to her in the town where she has lived her entire eighty–six years.

To my relief, Aunt Zeenie was sitting on the sofa in what she called her "front room," holding the receiver of her telephone in her hand. As she slowly turned her head from side to side, she was muttering, "She won't listen to me. She won't listen to me."

I gently took the receiver from her and sat on the stool at her feet. "Now tell me, Aunt Zeenie," I said, "just who is this person who won't listen to you?"

"It's that spiteful Mrs. Fletcher at the drug store," she said. "I only want to find out if my arthritis medicine is ready. But every time I dial the number, she butts right in and doesn't give me a chance to ask. All she says is for me to press button one if I want to refill a prescription, or press number two if I want information about when the store opens, and on and on like that."

Looking at me like a lost child, Aunt Zeenie said, "And I try to tell her that I don't have any buttons to press, but she doesn't listen to me."

"Aunt Zeenie," I said as I patted her shoulder, "that's only a recording; the drug store hasn't opened yet this morning." But Aunt Zeenie is right about one thing; she sure doesn't have any buttons to press. She still has a very old, dial–type telephone. I have offered more than once to have new push–button phones installed for her, but she insists she doesn't want to change. She remembers when all she had to do was lift the receiver and the operator would be right there to help. Most of the time she didn't even have to know the number of the person she was calling because the operator knew everyone in town.

It seems that every day Aunt Zeenie brings me a new challenge, and she is not even my real aunt. I didn't know this until I was in the third grade and had to draw my family tree. I was dismayed because I couldn't find a branch for Aunt Zeenie. Daddy said that was because I wasn't drawing a nut tree. My mother shamed him for saying such a thing and explained to me that addressing someone as aunt is just a southern custom, showing respect and honor. Until then I had never given a thought to the fact that just about everyone I knew called her Aunt Zeenie except for our new pastor who always shook her hand and asked, "How's Miss Poindexter this morning?" I thought he was asking about one of Aunt Zeenie's friends because I had never heard anyone call her by that name.

With no close relatives, Aunt Zeenie took it upon herself some years ago to adopt me as her care giver. She is sound of body for her age and fairly sound of mind, although she has a definite stubborn streak. As of late it has been her telephone that has given us a problem, or I should say, has given me a problem.

Recently she noticed her neighbors' dog had gotten out of their yard and was headed down the street. Since she knew the dog wasn't allowed to run loose, she thought she ought to let them know Old Shep was on the prowl. She related to me that she had dialed their number but before she had a chance to say anything, her neighbor interrupted and started right in telling her that they couldn't take a call just then, but if she would leave a number, they would return the call. Leave a number indeed! As long as she had known those folks, she had tried to be a good neighbor. If they were too busy to talk to her, then she wasn't about to leave her number. Their dog could just run away for all she cared!

Like most of us, Aunt Zeenie gets her share of telemarketing calls, usually right at the time she is having her evening meal. I told her the telephone company could fix her up with "Caller ID," and that way she would know whether or not she wanted to answer the phone. I wasn't sure, though, if this new equipment could be hooked up to her old dial telephone. No bother. She didn't want it anyway.

Another thing that gets Aunt Zeenie all riled up is to be talking on the phone with someone and right in the middle of their conversation, she will be told: "Wait just a minute while I answer this other line." I explained this is a special service, known as "Call Waiting" and is available through the phone company. She said as far as she is concerned whoever calls last should do the waiting and if it is more than a minute, she just hangs up. She is far too busy to waste her time.

Aunt Zeenie's memory isn't as good as it once was, but of course, neither is mine. Like her, I have a hard time remembering phone numbers, even those of my children. My husband solved that for me by putting in a new phone with a memory bank for ten of my most frequently dialed numbers. I showed Aunt Zeenie how great it is to just press "memo"and one number instead of having to remember and dial an entire phone number. I also demonstrated the redial feature. Her response was that anyone too busy to dial a number doesn't have time to be making phone calls anyway.

Finally realizing all my efforts were in vain, I decided to drop the whole issue. If the old dial telephone suited Aunt Zeenie, so be it! It was all right with me. I left her in the care of my twenty–year–old granddaughter and took a two–week vacation. I don't know what transpired between the two of them while I was gone, but when I returned I gave Aunt Zeenie a call. After two rings, I heard her say, "I may or may not be at home just now, but unless you are selling vinyl siding, wanting to clean my carpets, or sell me some life insurance, you can leave a message and your number. I'll return your call real soon—probably. If this is an emergency, you can reach me on my cell phone. Check with my granddaughter for the number."

HERALD OF SPRING

Winter's cold is almost gone,
A friend told me today;
He stopped to spread the tidings
That spring is on the way.

Quite a sassy one was he,
In his sleek red vest;
To sing of spring's arrival,
He really looked his best.

I saw him turn a time or two;
He whistled a happy tune,
As if to say his many friends
Would be arriving soon.

Sporty little friend of mine,
What a joy you bring.
In my heart I sing with you,
O Robin, herald of spring.

ANGELS IN DISGUISE

*I*t was 5:00 o'clock on a Friday afternoon—rush hour traffic time. I was driving a "loaner" car, having left my car at a garage for repair. I stopped for a traffic light at a busy intersection in one of the less desirable parts of our city. The light changed to green, but I didn't go. The loaner car had stalled several times as I tried to make my way home, but I had managed to beg it along. This time, however, it evidently had died completely. I could hear horns blaring in the line of cars behind me.

As tears filled my eyes, I saw two young men jump out of the pickup truck in the next lane. At another time, they might have frightened me. Long hair. Beards. Well worn, dirty clothing. One of them began directing traffic around my vehicle while the other raised the hood, soon advising that the problem was with the fuel pump. Taking complete control of the situation, the acting traffic director stood in the middle of the intersection and stopped traffic from all directions while the other man walked to the car directly behind me.

"You will have to push this stalled car across the street to the lot on the corner," he told the lady who was sitting impatiently in the driver's seat.

She was insistent she could not do that.

"Well, you will have to," he said, giving her no choice. Under his guidance, she inched up to the bumper of the old loaner and pushed the car to the indicated spot.

After moving their truck out of the street, the men began working on the fuel pump. Not having tools they needed, one of them went to a nearby automotive parts store and borrowed the necessary wrenches. I have since wondered what was said that caused the manager of that store to be willing to entrust his tools with a total stranger.

After working a short while, the men concluded that the fuel pump was beyond repair. They returned the borrowed tools and then offered to drive me to my home. I declined, saying I would call a friend to come for me. When I tried to pay them for coming to my rescue, they seemed almost insulted. I feel certain they could have used the money, but they wouldn't accept it. Smiling as they turned to leave, one of them said, "You'd spoil it all if you paid us."

When I am inclined to judge someone by his appearance, my thoughts go back to those two young men. To be sure, their outward appearance left much to be desired. Inside, where it really matters, they were beautiful. Angels in disguise? There is no doubt in my mind.

MISS BELLE
OF HOOTEN HOLLOW

Some of the old folks around Hooten Hollow remember when it was just a sleepy little Ozark town, hardly more than a wide place in the road. About the only excitement was on Saturday nights when the young men gathered at Papa Pete's combination cafe and pool hall, as he put it, "to hoot and holler." When the town finally got its own post office, there had been so much talk about "going to hoot and holler," they just made Hooten Hollow the official name. After all, as far as the local folks were concerned, the pronunciation didn't change.

Nowadays the fame of Hooten Hollow is the Ding–a–ling Band, the wonderful trout fishing, and Miss Belle. Actually, Miss Belle should have first billing because without her there would be no Ding–a–lings, nor would trout fishing likely have become such a profitable business.

Miss Belle came to Hooten Hollow as a bride a half century ago, more or less. No one knows her exact age and she has no intention of telling. There is talk among the old–timers, though, that she was a young widow who had vowed never to wed again. Then that handsome

Mike Murphy came along and swept her right off her feet and brought her to the town of Hooten Hollow.

It was Mike and Miss Belle who built the first motel in Hooten Hollow and worked up a campaign to attract tourists to the area. It was during the Great Depression of the 1930s. Times were hard for everybody. The local folks had their gardens. What they couldn't grow or buy with the butter–and–egg money, they just had to do without. That is, until the Murphys came to their rescue.

Before they got their motel open, Mike and Miss Belle were off to some of the big cities like Springfield and Little Rock, promoting fall foliage tours, spring flower tours, and summer float fishing in the clear lakes and rivers, and even the beauty and serenity of the winter months in the little valley between the mountains.

They did real well—on all except the winter wonderland stuff. Most people just aren't into getting snowed in somewhere, knowing the roads might be closed for a week or more, no matter how peaceful and pretty it is.

The motel had been open only a few months when Mike Murphy had a fatal heart attack. Most everyone feared Miss Belle would go back to her own family in Illinois, but she proved them wrong. The Murphy Motel had been her Mike's dream, and she intended to see that it was a success.

She worked up a marketing program and a long–range plan long before such things as business forecasting were even thought about. Of course, she didn't know she was doing anything innovative. She was just trying to fill those rooms.

Miss Belle ran ads in all the big city papers within a 500–mile radius of Hooten Hollow, promoting the beauty of the area and the wonderful trout fishing. Her weekend tourist packages included not only rooms at her motel, but also special deals for float fishing, which was beginning to get attention as far away as Chicago. Miss Belle would extol the wonders of floating the clear rivers, with experienced guides who would motor upstream, then keep the boat floating silently back down, allowing those fishing to cast off from the side of the boat. It was virtually guaranteed that everyone who fished would catch his limit, often before noon. Then came the real treat. The guides would dock in a shady cove and before you could say, "The big one got away," the fish fresh out of the lake would be cleaned, cooked in a skillet over a camp fire, and served along with greasy fried potatoes, pork–and–beans, a green salad, and canned peaches for dessert.

There was one thing that bothered Miss Belle when she bragged about the wonders of float fishing. She had never personally had such an experience. When her cousin Betty came for a visit, they decided the time had come. They were going float fishing.

Back then float fishing down the Buffalo and White Rivers was a sport that excluded women for the most part. Although Miss Belle was not aware of it at the time, when she called Bowe's Boat Dock to set up their float trip, none of the guides wanted the job. The fact is, they drew straws to see who would have to take the two ladies.

All the fellows were waiting at the dock the next morning to see if the ladies showed up. If they hadn't had so much respect for Miss Belle and weren't indebted to her for most of their float business, there probably would have been some real belly–laughing when those ladies stepped out of the car. Cousin Betty had on blue jeans and a plaid shirt, but this kind of outfit wasn't in Miss Belle's wardrobe.

Miss Belle was always the proper lady. For one thing, she wouldn't think of leaving home without wearing a girdle. So under that pretty blue one–piece jumpsuit, she was properly girdled down. Her blonde hair was stylishly pushed back under a flower–bedecked straw hat, and her leather ankle boots matched the tan and yellow scarf that protruded from her shirt pocket. She was ready for the big day on the river.

Actually, just as Miss Belle always said, fishing was good. Under the direction of the guide, who baited their hooks, showed them how to cast, and then took off the fish and rebaited for them, the ladies did real well. In fact, when all the boats docked for lunch, the men were beginning to show a little respect for the two, albeit reluctantly.

It was while the guides were cooking the fish and getting lunch ready that Miss Belle realized a one–piece jumpsuit isn't the appropriate attire for float fishing. "Over the hill and far away" is about the best way to describe toilet facilities along the river bank. The men took off to the left and the two ladies climbed a hill over to the right. The only way to describe what happened next is to say that with the one–piece jumpsuit and the tight girdle down around her ankles, Miss Belle sort of got overbalanced and down the hill she went, in a squatting position and waddling like a duck.

What followed depends on whose version you hear. But Miss Belle was a good sport. She bought some blue jeans, saved the jumpsuit for shopping trips, and threw away the girdle!

Although the Murphy Motel did well during fishing season, Miss Belle needed year–round business. That's how the Ding–a–lings got started. Hooten Hollow had become a mecca for retirees. Miss Belle decided to organize a senior citizens' band. It was a success from the start, beyond her wildest dreams. They were quite appropriately called the "Ding–a–lings." Some of the band members actually could play real instruments, such as the fiddle, banjo, flute, and keyboard. Others played cow bells, spoons, wash boards, combs, sticks tapped together—whatever they found to serve the purpose. They practiced at the Murphy Motel and often stayed for lunch or dinner. Many returned on Sunday for the noon buffet.

Miss Belle turned her seldom–used meeting room into a supper club. On Friday and Saturday nights the local folks came to eat and dance. Special entertainment was furnished by the Ding–a–lings. It might seem unbelievable, but they were good! They even received an invitation to play at one of the parties in Washington during the President's inauguration.

The thrill of the invitation was dimmed by the realization that there would be considerable expense involved. A bus would have to be chartered to get them there. Rooms in Washington would be very expensive. And, even oldies like to eat.

Once again, it was Miss Belle to the rescue!

She began planning a money–raising Thanksgiving dance, with all proceeds going toward the Ding–a–lings' Washington trip. Ads were run in daily and weekly papers for miles around. Posters went up in store windows. A banner stretched across the front of the courthouse. Band members sold advance tickets and sought cash donations and pledges from local businesses. Excitement spread like wildfire.

A special feature for the event was to be a dance contest. This, of course, was another of Miss Belle's ideas. She promised a Thanksgiving turkey to the winning couple.

The big night finally came. A crowd soon filled the motel's former meeting room, decorated with crepe paper streamers and cutout turkeys.

The dance contest commenced. Competition was fierce, but the final decision of the judges went to a young couple who jitter–bugged their way to the top. They would be the recipients of Miss Belle's Thanksgiving turkey, and they waited on the stage with the band, receiving the judges' congratulations, while Miss Belle went to get their prize.

The couple's expectation of a turkey that would be thawed and roasted for their Thanksgiving dinner left with the re-entrance of Miss Belle, not carrying a frozen turkey but leading a real, live gobbler. She held a long red ribbon attached to a little band around the turkey's neck. He followed along quite nicely—until the crowd realized what was happening. They clapped and cheered and stomped their feet.

The surprise of the winning couple was nothing compared to that of the turkey. Terrified by all the noise, he broke loose from Miss Belle's leash and took off flying around the room, squawking and flapping his wings. Feathers were falling, and that wasn't all! The people tried to cover their heads with their hands as they ran out of the room.

After the turkey finally was caught, the tables and chairs wiped clean, and the floor swept and mopped, the folks came back in and the party resumed.

Poor Miss Belle! She kept saying, "But I practiced walking in with the turkey and he did just great." She just hadn't considered the action of the crowd and the reaction of the turkey!

All in all, the evening was a success. Enough money was raised to send the Ding–a–lings to Washington. The turkey lived happily ever after at a neighbor's farm because the winning couple refused to accept him. Best of all, Miss Belle celebrated Thanksgiving with a full house at the Murphy Motel.

LIGHTS ALONG THE WAY

My mother told me stories
As she tucked me into bed.
This was a nightly ritual
Before my prayers were said.

In school I listened eagerly
To stories my teacher told,
Of kings and queens and palaces,
And knights in days of old.

My young imagination soared;
I lived the stories heard.
I became a gallant warrior,
Mighty giant, or tiny bird.

Throughout my adulthood
Are stories of every kind;
Some read for pleasure only;
Others enrich my mind.

Now within my golden years,
Stories brighten every day,
Emerging from my memory—
My lights along the way.

BONNIE ROSE

B onnie Rose was a very sad little girl. She never wore a happy face.

She lived in a pretty red brick house. She had a wonderful mother and father and four big brothers who loved her very much. She had a dog named Barney and a cat named Patches. She had her own room and lots of dolls and a shelf filled with all kinds of books. But Bonnie Rose was not a happy little girl.

She went to a brand new school, only a few blocks from her house. It was a beautiful school, with pink walls and bright colors in all the classrooms. Miss Smith was a wonderful teacher, and Bonnie Rose liked the girls in her room. But she didn't like the boys very much. That was part of the reason she was not happy. The boys teased her.

Bonnie Rose was sure everything would be better if only she had a different name. She didn't know another girl with a name like Bonnie Rose. The four other girls who sat at her table were named Allison and Jennifer and Joanna and Amanda. They had nice names, and they had nicknames too. Sometimes Allison was called Al, and Jennifer was Jen. Lots of people called Joanna "Jo Jo" and most everyone called Amanda "Mandy." She didn't have a nickname, although sometimes her daddy called her "Rosie" and would sing a little song he made up about "Sweet Rosie is My Pretty Posey." She thought Rosie was even worse than Bonnie Rose.

It really was all her mother's fault because she was the one who had named her. Her father said he always gave that job to her mother because he wasn't good at names. Her mother hadn't done too bad with names for her brothers. She couldn't understand why she hadn't picked out a better name for her.

Her oldest brother was named Robert, although most of his friends called him Bob or Bobby. At home he usually was called Bubba. That was because when Norris, who was her next–to–the–oldest brother, was learning to talk, he couldn't say "brother" and it sounded like "Bubba."

After Robert and Norris, the next baby was named Adam. Bonnie Rose really liked that name even if she never called him Adam. He was big and strong and liked to play football. His friends said he could run down the football field very fast, charging ahead like a buffalo. So they gave him the name "Buffalo." It soon was shortened to just Buff, which is what Bonnie Rose always called him.

Her youngest brother was named Frank, but everyone called him Nip. He got that nickname from his brothers because his black curly hair was always tangled. When their mother combed his hair, he would cry and say she was pulling his nips. The other boys thought this was funny and began calling him Nip.

With four boys already, her mother was sure the fifth baby would be another boy. She had the name picked out. She was going to name this one John.

What a surprise! She had a baby girl. But she didn't have any names picked out for a girl. Maybe she would name her for Grandmother Dora. But Grandmother Dora didn't like that idea. She said when she was a little girl, the boys at school would tease her and call her Dumb Dora and she wasn't dumb at all. Grandmother Dora said to please not give her that name.

Maybe she would name her for Aunt Mary. Mother thought that would make Aunt Mary very happy.

"Oh, no," said Aunt Mary, "please don't name your pretty baby for me." Aunt Mary said when she was a little girl, the boys at school liked to tease her and say, "Mary, Mary, quite contrary, how does your garden grow?" Just like in the nursery rhyme. "Besides," said Aunt Mary, "there are a lot of girls named Mary. Give your baby a name that is different."

Of course Bonnie Rose knew how she finally got her name. She had been told about that since she was just a baby. Her daddy was so happy to have a little girl, and he loved her mother so much. He bought her mother a dozen beautiful pink roses. Mama said she had looked at her baby's tiny little mouth, pink and sort of puckered up like a little pink rose bud, and she said, "I will name her Rose." Because Mama thought she was so pretty, she chose the name Bonnie, which means beautiful. Bonnie Rose.

Bonnie Rose didn't like her name and she certainly didn't think of herself as beautiful. She wished she looked more like her brothers. They all had brown eyes and dark hair, just like Daddy. In the summer when they were outside a lot, they all got wonderful suntans.

She was just like her mother. She had blue eyes and blond hair and had to put on lots of suntan lotion when she went to the beach and always wear a big hat to keep the sun from shining on her face. She never got a suntan. She got freckles.

She hated her freckles even more than she hated her name. At recess, the boys would call out, "Bonnie Rose, Bonnie Rose, you've got freckles on your nose!" And she would cry.

Her mother tried to tell her that her freckles made her pretty, but she still hated them. She did feel bad, though, when her mother reminded her that she had freckles, too. Bonnie Rose certainly didn't think her mother was ugly. She was just about the most beautiful mother anyone ever had. And she guessed it made her mother sort of sad when she said she hated her name because it was her mother who had named her.

Then one day right after the Christmas holidays a new family moved into the white house at the end of Bonnie Rose's street. There was a girl who was just Bonnie Rose's age and was in her room at school. The girl's name was Lily!

Bonnie Rose wondered if Lily's mother had thought her baby looked like a Lily when she was born. It almost made her giggle, but she didn't say anything because she didn't want to hurt Lily's feelings.

She was sure she knew why her name wasn't Bonnie Lily. She probably wasn't pretty when she was born because Bonnie Rose didn't think Lily was pretty now. In fact, Bonnie Rose thought, she looks a lot like me. Her hair is blonde, and her eyes are blue. We are almost the same size, but Lily has lots more freckles.

There was another big difference, too. Lily always wore a happy face.

At first some of the boys teased Lily and called her Freckle Face, but Lily never cried. In fact, she laughed right with them. She said she had moved there from the country, where her father had a dairy farm. She said one of his cows had spit bran in her face! That made all the boys and girls laugh. Soon no one teased her at all and everyone wanted to be her "best friend."

When they were walking to school one morning, Bonnie Rose asked Lily how she could always be so happy, especially with so many freckles. And didn't she just hate having the same name as a flower?

Lily said she used to wish her name was Sandra or Kathy like one of her cousins, but she really didn't mind being Lily. She had been born on Easter Sunday, and her mother had been given a pot of beautiful Easter lilies. They had filled the room with their sweet perfume and were so lovely, and of course, that is how she got her name.

"Just think," said Lily, "suppose I had been born on Christmas. Someone might have brought my mother a pot of poinsettias, the beautiful red Christmas flowers. Think what my mother might have named me then! I would much rather be named Lily than Poinsettia." This made both girls laugh.

Lily told Bonnie Rose that for a long time she didn't like her freckles. She had scrubbed them with kitchen cleanser and once even tried fingernail polish remover, which had made blisters on her face. She had washed her face with lemon juice because someone had told her that would bleach out her freckles, but that didn't work either.

Then her favorite uncle had come to visit them, and he had told her how much he liked her freckles and how he had wanted freckles when he was a little boy. He had said that freckles are just kisses from angels. Of course, she knew that wasn't really true, but she liked to pretend it was.

Her uncle told her that it really doesn't matter how one looks on the outside. The important thing is how one is on the inside and how one acts.

Bonnie Rose thought about that a lot after she had gone to bed that night. She really had not understood what her grandmother meant when she often would say, "Pretty is as pretty does." Now she knew. It means that you are pretty if you act pretty. No matter how pretty you look, if you don't act nice, you won't have friends and no one will like you. That must be right because Lily wasn't a very pretty girl, just to look at her, but once you got to know her, you really, really liked her. You didn't even think about how she looked. You just saw her big smile and heard her happy laugh. And you loved her a lot when she gave you a big hug or held your hand as you walked to school.

Bonnie Rose went to sleep with a happy feeling and a smile on her face because she had decided that she would try to be like her best friend Lily.

The next day Miss Smith asked all the boys and girls to take turns standing in front of the class and telling what makes them happy.

Joe was happy because his father was going to take him fishing on Saturday. Billy was going camping. Joyce had a new dress that had pink flowers on the skirt, and she was going to wear it to her cousin's wedding. Paul was happy because his mother had bought him a new fish for his aquarium.

Soon it was time for those at Bonnie Rose's table. Allison said she was happy because she was going to have a birthday party the next week. Jennifer was happy because she was going on an airplane, all by herself, to visit her grandparents in Florida. Joanna's cat had five new kittens and that made her happy. Amanda's mother was going to take her to the zoo on Saturday.

Then Miss Smith said, "Bonnie Rose, tell us what makes you happy."

Bonnie Rose almost danced as she hurried to the front of the room. She looked at Lily and with a big smile, she said:

> "I'm happy because my name is Bonnie Rose,
> And I have freckles on my nose."

UNCLE NIP

Neatly lettered on the mailbox at the side of a gravel road is the name FRANK HALL. That's the real name of the elderly gentleman who is better known to family and friends as "Uncle Nip." He and his wife moved from Memphis, Tenn., to rural Arkansas to enjoy the peace and quiet of country living. They planted fruit and nut–bearing trees, preserved vegetables from their garden, and cleared undergrowth in the wooded area of their twenty–acre retreat. Working together, side–by–side, they mowed grass, weeded flowerbeds, and cut wood for both the kitchen cook stove and the living room heater.

For twenty years Uncle Nip and his devoted wife of more than fifty–five years enjoyed their Arkansas home, sharing the workload and enjoying the fruits of their labor, before she lost her battle with lung cancer.

Uncle Nip's one remaining sibling, a sister, lives 200 miles from him and there are no other close relatives. Although he is blessed with wonderful neighbors, they are not within "hollering distance." This causes some of his friends to be concerned about his isolation. What most people do not understand, however, is that he is not really alone. Recorded in the book of Genesis, there was a man named Enoch, a righteous man, who walked with God. Uncle Nip is very much like Enoch.

On two occasions Uncle Nip had a flat tire on his pickup truck. The first time was when he was driving to his older sister's funeral. Before he had gotten out of the truck, a car stopped and the driver came to his assistance, quickly changing the tire. Uncle Nip's offer to pay was refused. The Good Samaritan shook hands, said "God bless you" and drove away. The second time was shortly before his wife's death. He was driving home from the hospital where she had undergone treatment and was concerned that her oxygen tank was nearly empty. When he realized his truck had a flat tire, he pulled to the shoulder of the highway. As before, almost immediately a car stopped. A man got out, changed the tire and refused to accept pay. He extended his hand and said, "God bless you" as he turned to leave. The same man? Uncle Nip wonders.

Another unusual "happening" involved his wife during the final month of her life. Almost totally bedridden, she awoke one night feeling chilled and sensed she was not alone although she knew Uncle Nip was asleep in another room. Within minutes he was at her bedside, covering her with an additional blanket. "How did you awake just when I needed you?" she asked. "How could I sleep when my leg was being pulled?" he answered.

Unlike most people who live in the country, Uncle Nip doesn't have chickens or cows or other animals. Prior to his wife's death, however, there was a very unfriendly cat that ventured as close as the back door of their house for daily handouts. Tiger, as they named him, never came near enough to be touched. That changed after Uncle Nip's wife died. As though Tiger sensed an emptiness in the home, he soon began appearing on the front porch to wait for his meals. Not many weeks passed until the cat felt comfortable enough to come inside the house. Although he still prowled the neighborhood at night, many daytime hours were spent curled up in Uncle Nip's lap. They enjoyed each other's company for several years, but Tiger liked his independence. His overnight wanderings began stretching to two or three days, and eventually he left for good.

Uncle Nip had a similar experience with a dog that he appropriately called Mutt. Although he never allowed Mutt inside the house, they became close outdoor friends. Unfortunately, Mutt had a wild side that was never conquered and which resulted in his numerous fights with other animals. He also was the victim of gunshot wounds. Uncle Nip never knew who fired the shots or whether they were accidental or intentional, but he nursed the dog until he had recovered with only a limp in one hind leg. Mutt's untimely death brought another heartache, but the void was partially filled by Muffin.

Muffin is a small shaggy dog that belongs to the neighboring family, about a quarter of a mile from Uncle Nip's house. At first she only visited with him when her own folks were at work or at school. It wasn't long, though, until she was sleeping in his garage and waiting on his porch for her breakfast.

Although Uncle Nip claims Muffin is nothing but a nuisance, it is known that his weekly grocery list now includes chicken, which he cooks and adds to her dog food (which he also buys) to make it more tasty.

Being legally deaf, much of what Uncle Nip says he "hears" comes from an inner source and is not amplified by the two hearing aids he wears. On an early morning as he walked across his back yard, he "heard" a voice asking, "Do you know you have lost your wallet?" He slapped the back pocket where his wallet should have been. It was empty. He searched his house, looking beneath the sofa pillows and under furniture. He looked in his truck, in the garage and in the yard where he had been mowing the grass. After two days, he decided he would have to drive into town and get replacements for his lost driver's license and Medicare card. As he sat on the side of his bed, putting on his shoes, he again "heard" a voice. He was instructed to "look down." His reply was that he already had looked under the bed and his wallet was not there. Again he was told to "look down." He audibly replied, "That is ridiculous—there is nothing on the floor under my bed!" But being so instructed the third time, he looked down and he saw his wallet—not on the floor, but on the bed rail!

Relating another experience, Uncle Nip said, "I was coming in from the woods on the tractor and wasn't as careful as I should have been. I went under a low–hanging limb that struck me in the face and knocked off my glasses. I went back and searched everywhere in the vicinity of where the limb smacked me, but found nothing. Although I can see fairly well at a distance without glasses, I decided to go to the house and get my other pair before continuing the search."

Wearing his spare glasses, he started out of the house. "Then I thought that the thing I should have done in the first place was to ask the One who knew where the glasses were to tell me. So I prayed and said, 'Now, Lord, I need those glasses so I am asking you to show me where they are.' I then got on the tractor and went back, confident I would find the glasses. I saw them in the weeds beside the driveway even before I had gotten off of the tractor to look for them."

Uncle Nip prays expecting an answer, but not necessarily a miracle. And he has learned that his time and God's time are not always the same. Recently he found a hearing aid that he had lost nine months earlier. He was in his orchard and leaned to pick up a plum that had fallen from one of the trees. Beside the plum, almost buried in mud, was his hearing aid. Although he had little hope that it still would be useable, he gave it a thorough cleaning and put in a new battery. Then he had a conversation with the Lord.

"Lord, I can't say that I need this hearing aid because I have two that I wear, plus one spare. I know it was a miracle that I even found it, but a second miracle would be nice." He put the tiny mechanism into his ear and flipped the switch. No, it wasn't working. After further cleaning, he tried it again and heard a faint humming sound, but nothing more. He laid it aside and a few hours later he tried it again. "Then it came on loud and clear," he said, "better than when it was brand new."

Uncle Nip says he continues his regular chores, cutting wood, mowing grass and taking care of all the usual things that need attention, but he admits to moving at a slower pace now that he has celebrated his 87th birthday.

His days always begin with a good breakfast—hot cooked cereal, two or three pieces of toast with butter and jelly, fruit juice and one cup of coffee. Before every meal he gives thanks for what has been provided and his daily schedule includes both morning and evening Bible reading and meditation.

In many ways Uncle Nip has become a creature of habit, one being that every Monday morning he fills the old wringer washing machine and two rinse tubs and does his weekly laundry. Linens and white clothes go in first, then colored items, and lastly his overalls. Except in inclement weather, everything is hung on wire lines that stretch across the back yard. When it is raining or the temperature is below freezing, he makes use of the lines on his enclosed back porch.

Tuesday is ironing day. Although his late wife ironed everything, including towels and washcloths, Uncle Nip has found it more to his liking to "fold and store," except where wrinkles persist on his shirts and trousers.

Although Uncle Nip doesn't claim to be an authority on miracles, he does offer this bit of advice: "You won't get a miracle unless you believe one is possible and you have to make your requests known." He talks to the Lord, not only before every meal and at bedtime, but also throughout the day. Perhaps more important, he listens to the Lord. According to Uncle Nip, "You have to stay tuned in."

He should know because, like Enoch, he walks with the Lord.

THANK YOU, FATHER, FOR THIS STAY

*K*neeling beside his bed at he said his nightly prayers, five–year–old Matthew paused and turned his eyes toward his grandmother. *Touching her gently on her arm as she knelt beside him, he whispered, "Nannie, what's a stay?"*

The child's eyes revealed the faith he had in his grandmother's ability to explain the meaning of this troubling word. She and his grandfather had provided a loving home for him since shortly after his birth. To him they were all knowledge and power. If it is true that children learn by asking questions, thought the grandmother, my grandson will be among the top in his class when he enters kindergarten this year. It seemed to her Matthew's questions were endless. Usually, however, she was able to give answers that satisfied him. This time she was puzzled.

"What's a stay?" he had asked.

Attempting to explain, his grandmother said, "It's like you stay with your Pappy and me. This is your home. You don't go away; you live here. You stay."

It was obvious her explanation did not satisfy the child. The corners of his mouth turned down in a pout. "No, Nannie," he said, "that's not the kind of stay I'm talking about."

"Well," said his grandmother, "you will have to tell me what kind of stay you mean."

With downcast eyes, Matthew explained, "When I am at Uncle Ronnie's, my cousins take turns saying the blessing at breakfast every morning and they always say, 'Thank you God for this stay,' and I don't know what a stay is."

Smiling on the inside, but careful not to let her amusement show, this loving grandmother pulled the child close to her and explained that his little cousins simply talk too fast and actually are saying, "Thank you for this day."

Saying softly, "Thank you for this day" several times, Matthew looked up at his grandmother with an impish grin. He gave her a quick hug as he climbed into his bed, no longer concerned about a stay. But his grandmother pondered the question as she kissed him goodnight. She considered that it might be more appropriate to thank God for the stay than for the day. She had explained to Matthew that stay means not leaving...to be there, and that's how God is. Jesus said, "Lo, I am with you alway, even until the end of the world." Through the Holy Spirit, He stays with those who would keep Him near.

Yes, Matthew's little cousins had said it right. It is good to thank God for every new day, but even more important, to thank Him for His constant stay.

A HOUSE NOT HER OWN

Martha stood at the top of the staircase and sighed as she looked down at the magnificent rooms on either side of the center hall. For four years her family had lived here, since the spring of 1861 when her son had answered the call for men to fight in defense of the newly established Confederacy. Never had she dreamed of living in such spacious surroundings. She still was awed by the fourteen–foot ceilings and the tall windows through which she could step onto the porches that wrapped around the sides and front of the house. Yet to her this was nothing more than just the place where she and Lawrence and their children had been living for the past four years. It was not her home, nor did she have any desire for such splendor. She longed to be back in Todd County, Kentucky, in the little house Lawrence had built for her when they were married more than 33 years ago.

Martha never had wanted to be anything except the wife of Lawrence Hall and the mother of his children. Life had been good on their little farm. The boys, Richard and James, had worked with their father in the fields. Their oldest daughter had married her childhood sweetheart and had given them a grandson who was a delight beyond measure.

Her family had been so closely knit. She had thought nothing could ever come between her and her brothers and their extended families. They had worked together and played together. There had been barn–raisings and quilting parties, hay–balings and square dances. Decades earlier they had built the little white frame church where they all gathered every Sunday for worship services.

The last four years had been painful. First there were arguments and angry debates among members of her family concerning southern nationalism. Her brothers had taken a strong stand against slavery, while her Lawrence held fast to his opposing convictions. With the election of Abraham Lincoln to the Presidency, the gulf between them had widened. It still was difficult for Martha to accept the fact that the ones she loved so dearly had become virtual enemies in the great Civil War, brother fighting against brother.

Their son Richard had just celebrated his twentieth birthday when the war began. How well she remembered that morning at breakfast when he had announced that he was leaving to join Morgan's Kentucky Raiders, the cavalry unit led by General John Hunt Morgan. The little girls had cried and begged him not to go. Her own hot tears had dampened her pillow many nights, but Lawrence had been proud of their son. No doubt he himself would have volunteered had it not been that he was needed to care for his family, especially now that both neighbors and kin felt them to be traitors.

The decision to move south had not been an easy one, but even the children were being affected by their brother's departure. The school where once they had looked forward to attending had become a dreaded place where they were taunted by the other boys and girls.

Martha remembered how heavy her heart was as she had packed their personal belongings and what furniture and household items they were able to bring with them. The wagon had been so heavily loaded, she wondered how the horses had been able to pull it. It was an exciting adventure for the children, but what a heartbreaking experience for her—and for Lawrence too.

They were tired and in need of baths when they arrived in Memphis and were most fortunate to have found a place to rent. The 10–room house on the 5,000–acre plantation was available only because the owners did not wish to live so far out from the city in such turbulent times. The house was only nine years old, having been built in 1852 by Samuel and Joseph Mosby. With a brick foundation, weatherboard siding and a slate-covered gable roof, it was both eye–catching and durable.

Although Martha had never met Mrs. Mosby, she felt a certain kinship, both having left their homes because of the war. Maybe soon they could return.

The war was over now. General Lee had surrendered. If only she would receive some word from Richard. He had been wounded in the Battle of Vicksburg and had spent 18 months imprisoned in Rock Island, Ill. Some months earlier they had received a letter from one of his fellow inmates, informing them that Richard was being moved to Richmond, Va. as an exchange prisoner. They had heard nothing more.

Martha wondered if she should begin packing for the trip back to Kentucky. How would they be accepted by their families and former neighbors? Would Richard expect to find them still in Memphis or in Todd County? Had he been given a release?

These were questions that seemed to have no answers.

As she wiped a tear on the corner of her apron, she prayed for divine guidance in the decisions she and Lawrence must make very soon.

It was while she was yet standing at the top of the staircase that the front door was slowly opened. Although Martha was not one to be easily frightened, a chill ran down her spine as she faced the tall young man. His clothing was dirty, tattered, and hanging loosely from his thin body. A heavy dark beard concealed most of his face and his shoulder–length hair hung in a mass of tangles. As he stared up into her face, his eyes glistened and the corners of his mouth turned up in a slight smile. There was something familiar about this man, yet Martha did not recognize him. It was old Sport who ran to greet his master, barking joyfully to welcome him home.

Richard had made the long walk from Richmond, Virginia to Memphis. He was home at last from a war that had not ended as he had wished. He was, nevertheless, more fortunate than many. Some of his friends had lost arms or legs; others had lost their lives.

Martha ran down the stairs with outreached arms. The tears streaming down her face were those of joy and thanksgiving for the return of Richard Robert Redford Hall, her son—my grandfather.

GARAGE SALE ADDICT

Appropriately attired in faded blue jeans, bright tee shirt that reads, "Garage Sale Goddess" (a gift from my daughter–in–law), comfortable shoes, and fanny pack belted around my waist, I'm ready for my weekly jaunt. It's early Saturday morning and I am a garage sale addict, out to find treasures that others have trashed.

I didn't become an addict overnight. In fact, I once laughed at a neighbor who had this same addiction. My illness, as some believe this to be, came on slowly. It began when I went to a "moving sale" at the end of our street and found some wonderful bargains—a lawn chair that needed only new plastic webbing, a stool with a missing leg (which I was sure my husband Felix could repair), and a pair of denim shorts that would be a perfect fit if I lost another five pounds.

The following weekend there was a rummage sale at our church. I was amazed at the almost–new things some people discard. I bought a very good ironing board for three dollars. The one I have been using for years probably will last my lifetime, but I thought my granddaughter would need one when she moves into her own apartment after she finishes college. I also purchased a nice sports coat for Felix. It was navy blue with brown top stitching and a real bargain. He just shook his head and said surely I must have noticed that no well–dressed man wears polyester these days.

I couldn't resist the bag of wooden clothespins. At least two dozen for just a quarter! I always have felt that clothes hung outside to dry in the sunshine have a clean, fresh smell. I was sure I could talk Felix into setting a couple of poles in concrete and stringing a line between them. No one had told me that outside clotheslines are not allowed in our neighborhood.

I really got the "bug" when I went with a friend to a big community–wide sale. I was totally fascinated by the wonderful things that could be bought at such bargain prices. Carports and garages, on street after street, were filled with tables of practically everything anyone could want. It had not taken me long to learn that need has nothing to do with what one buys at a yard sale. (Incidentally, the terms "garage sale," "yard sale," and "carport sale" are interchangeable. In the classified advertising section of the newspaper, all are listed under "Garage Sales.")

In the beginning I limited myself to shopping a maximum of three hours each Saturday morning. I would then rush home to have a late breakfast with my husband. I had, of course, fortified myself with coffee and toast before heading out. Gradually I increased my allotted time until finally we were sharing lunch instead of breakfast.

In order to use my carporting time more efficiently, I began studying the classified ads. On Fridays I would make a list of all the sales in the affluent community a few miles east of our home. Then I would work out the exact route to be taken, noting the hour each sale was scheduled to open. Experience had taught me that most sales begin earlier than advertised. This happens because eager bargain hunters often are knocking or banging on garage doors at the crack of dawn. I haven't stooped to that, however, as I feel it is not ethical—nor fair to other prospective buyers.

I also have discovered that there are certain people who regularly hold garage sales. I avoid locations where I have noticed sales are held about once a month. I don't believe people clean out their attics that often. It's my contention that these sales are run by "professionals" who search out carport bargains to later sell at jacked–up prices.

One might surmise that only women are attracted to garage sales, but men too know there are bargains to be had. They are good prospects for the larger items, such as lawn mowers, chain saws, barbecue grills, furniture, appliances, etc. Children also can be seen at sales, usually grumbling because they would rather be at home watching cartoons on television. Some of the youngsters have a few nickels and dimes and are learning the fine art of carporting from their mothers, who I suspect brought them along because they didn't have a sitter.

Recently Felix commented on the row of golf shoes he noticed on my closet shelf. That was easy to explain. I happened upon a sale where I found a dozen pairs of women's golf shoes...a much more expensive brand than I ever had purchased. Not only were they my exact size, but they appeared to have been hardly worn. The owner, a professional golfer, explained that she always bought a new pair each time she participated in a tournament and simply had too many to keep. Five dollars a pair was an unbelievable price! But I disciplined myself and bought only three pairs. With the two pairs I already had, I figured my stock of golf shoes would outlast me.

I also have been fortunate to find good canvas shoes, never paying more than a dollar and often only fifty cents a pair. I have red, blue, black, purple, white (three pairs), as well as plaid and striped shoes. Throw them in the washer with detergent and a good disinfectant and they are almost good as new.

Hats are another of my passions, and I have at least a dozen that I have bought at garage sales. Unfortunately, I don't wear hats—at least not often. I did wear one two years ago at the Storyteller's League luncheon, and I have considered wearing a hat next time I go on one of those fancy garden club tours. I may even decide to wear one to church if I quit singing in the choir. In the meantime, it gives me a good feeling to know I am prepared if a "hat occasion" should come along.

I'm a bit overstocked on dishes too. I've bought two full sets at yard sales. The first set was fine china—white with tiny pink flowers. The lady said it had been stored in her attic since her mother–in–law gave it to them as a wedding present. She didn't like the dishes or her mother–in–law, so the price was right. (Later I saw a similar set for several hundred dollars at an estate sale.) The other dishes were of lesser quality, but I couldn't pass up twelve place settings for twenty dollars. The "asking price" actually was thirty dollars, but carport prices are meant to be negotiated.

I have found too if the sale is about to close, prices may be cut as much as fifty percent. Sometimes there is no cost if the sellers are too tired to pack up what's left. I really did not want the oversized silk tree, which the man insisted he could load into my hatchback car. He had to tie down the trunk lid, but I got home with most of the leaves intact. I dragged it to the attic and later sold it for five dollars. About once a year I get overstocked with my carport purchases and I have to hold a sale myself. Forgetting where I got all the stuff displayed on my bargain tables, I say to Felix, "It's absolutely amazing what some people will buy!"

HAPPINESS IS A PATCHWORK QUILT

Happiness is a patchwork quilt,
Spread beneath a tree,
And not a soul within a mile—
Just my friend and me.
Here we sit and reminisce
About the joys we've shared—
Little things that mean a lot
Because somebody cared.
We listen to a robin sing
And feel a cool breeze blow.
We marvel at God's wonders
In whispers soft and low.
Happiness is a patchwork quilt
On a day in early spring;
All alone we sit and dream
Of what the years will bring.

BEVERLY'S BAKE SHOP

The lettering on the sign above the door boldly proclaims in bright blue and gold: *BEVERLY'S BAKE SHOP*. Twelve years ago this would have been a joke. Today it is a reality. While the town of Wagville doesn't have an annual watermelon festival, cotton carnival, or even a rattlesnake roundup, it has the best cakes, pies, and other baked goods for miles around.

Located on the town square, next to the hardware store, Beverly's Bake Shop is the gathering place for old and young alike who want to satisfy their sweet tooth or sweeten their disposition. It's often referred to as the town's "body and soul shop," because not only does Beverly sell the most delectable breads and pastries, but her cheerful smile and warm greeting are better than sunshine on a rainy day.

This charming lady is quick to credit her success in the baking business to her husband Gary. It wasn't that he gave her tricks of the trade or family recipes. Nor has he ever ventured into the kitchen to lend a hand. What he did was laugh. Beverly admits that she laughed too, most of the time, but her many early baking failures only made her more determined to succeed. Also she got tired of hearing about all the blue ribbons her mother–in–law had won at the county fair for her blackberry cake and maple sugar cookies.

It all began when Beverly, then a bride of less than three months, decided to bake her mother a birthday cake. Following the directions on the box, she mixed the batter and distributed it evenly in two greased and floured cake pans, placing them in the preheated oven as instructed. What could be more simple!

The problem began when the timer indicated the cake was done and she opened the oven door. Neither she nor her highly educated husband could figure out how to get the cake out of the pans.

In desperation, she phoned her mother–in–law. "Just put the pans on a rack until the cake cools a bit, then turn the pans upside down and the cake should come right out," she was told.

"I can't do that," Beverly lamented, "because the cake is about two inches above the top of the pans and sort of wrapped around the edges. I need help."

When her mother–in–law arrived she found Beverly in tears and Gary in uncontrollable laughter. The cake looked like two oversize, golden brown mushrooms, the tops of which had to be cut off to remove them from the pans. Beverly learned lesson number one. Never bake an angel food cake in regular eight-inch cake pans.

For their six–month anniversary, Beverly wanted to surprise her husband with old–fashioned tea cakes, his all–time favorite since childhood. His mother was pleased to be asked for her recipe and assured Beverly there was no way she could go wrong. Gary's surprise was genuine, especially when he took the first bite—or tried to.

"Beverly," he said, "these tea cakes look great and will be wonderful for target practice." They spent the afternoon in the country. The tea cakes were a good substitute for clay pigeons.

When their first daughter was about three years old, Beverly decided the two of them should bake Christmas cookies. Perhaps this would be the beginning of a family tradition. They would bake sugar cookies, decorate them with red and green candies, and take them to shut–ins in their neighborhood. In the middle of the process, she phoned her mother–in–law.

"I'm out of flour," she said, "so will it be all right if I roll out the dough in baking powder?"

"No, no, that will never do," she was told. "Maybe you could borrow some flour from your next–door neighbor."

Beverly didn't think she should do that since she already had borrowed the egg she needed. She did take her mother–in–law's next suggestion, however, and rolled the dough in pancake mix—not ideal but better than baking powder. The cookies looked better than they tasted. Their dog seemed to prefer the red ones, but he had learned to consume a variety of imperfections. Gary affirmed that they had the only dog in the neighborhood that begged for Alka–Seltzer.

Over the next several years, Beverly tried many recipes, several of which turned out well. Pecan pie wasn't one of them; however her father kept sending pecans from his trees in Louisiana. It must be true that practice makes perfect because she finally perfected it, along with many other delectable desserts.

Opening a shop was never in Beverly's plans. It just seemed the practical thing to do. The more she excelled in baking, the more she was asked to bake. Teachers suggested to her children that they bring their mother's cupcakes for all the class parties. Could she furnish ten dozen cookies for the reception at the new library?

Just for fun, she took a class in cake decorating at the local college. She soon was getting requests for wedding and birthday cakes. Subsequently she bought special bakeware, a new mixer and had a second oven installed.

Her husband no longer laughed at her baking efforts. She found it hard to believe how many people in his office were having birthdays, for which he needed her to bake a cake. His supply reached an end when she learned he was taking orders and selling her cakes.

At the urging of friends, Beverly entered several cakes in the Mid–South Fair competition. On the day of the judging, she and her mother drove to the fairgrounds early that morning in order to locate a good parking spot. Finding blue ribbons on three of her cakes put them in the mood for celebrating, and they spent the entire day touring the fair, enjoying the exhibits and feasting on corn dogs and cotton candy.

When both energy and money dwindled, and their feet ached, they decided it was time to head for home. They found the parking lot, but not their car. The lot that had been almost vacant when they arrived that morning now had every space filled. They walked up one lane and down the next, but their car seemed to have disappeared.

Finally, too tired to walk farther, they sat on the curb and cried. That's where one of Beverly's neighbors found them. His offer to drive them through the lot was readily accepted, and from the back seat of his car, they soon spotted the misplaced vehicle. In appreciation for his assistance, Beverly baked him a cake.

It was this cake that led to the opening of Beverly's Bake Shop.

"You should be in the bakery business," the neighbor said to Beverly when they happened to meet the following week at the Boy Scout Jamboree. "That was the best cake I have ever eaten." He urged her to look at a store being vacated on the town square. He felt it would be the perfect location for a bake shop.

As Beverly took another tray of blueberry muffins from the oven, she saw a line of customers waiting at the door for her shop to open—customers waiting to buy her products. She still furnishes cupcakes for school parties, cookies for receptions, and cakes for birthdays and other occasions...but for a price. And her husband no longer makes jokes about her baking. Nowadays she is the one who does the laughing—all the way to the bank.

THE CHRISTMAS ROBE

As I have done every Christmas morning for more than twenty years, I slip into the long, white flannel robe. The soft wool warms both my body and soul, giving me the wonderful feeling of being wrapped in love. It's a beautiful robe, which I wear only on special occasions, so it still has a like–new look.

My daughter Janet was seventeen the year I received it. A freshman in college, she had come home for the Christmas holidays. After several whispered conversations with her two brothers, she asked to borrow my car to go shopping.

"Drive carefully," I said as I gave her the keys, "and don't forget we all agreed to be very frugal with our Christmas spending." The children knew that since their father's death, our family operated on a rather tight budget. There weren't many gifts under our tree that year, and none was so big as the brightly wrapped box with the tag reading, "To Mom, from all of us."

Christmas morning we gathered around the tree in the living room. The children insisted I open their present first, handing me the big box. An array of emotions swept over me as I opened their gift and found the most beautiful robe I had ever seen, much less owned—soft white flannel with pink embroidered roses cascading down the shawl–type collar and along the cuffs of the sleeves.

"Put it on, Mom, and see how it fits," Janet insisted, "I would have gotten a small size but you always complain about your arms being long, so I got the large size so the sleeves would fit."

I was 5'2" and weighed 110 pounds. The sleeves were fine. The bottom of the robe dragged the floor at least four inches as I paraded around the room in my finery, but never had I received anything I liked and appreciated more. I knew from the label and the store tag that the robe was expensive—certainly more than my children could readily afford, but I couldn't reprimand them for their extravagance. Their joy in giving was apparent, and I could only thank them for such a beautiful present.

I carefully removed the robe, folded it, and replaced it in the box. "This is too beautiful to wear while I am preparing dinner," I told the children, "and besides, I want to leave it under the tree so I can show it to our guests when they arrive."

The day Janet went back to school, I headed for the shopping center. At the store where I knew the robe had been purchased, I went directly to the lingerie department in the hope that there would be a similar robe in a small size. It was my plan that Janet would never know I had made an exchange.

I found several robes in the same style, white with pink roses, identical to mine. In fact, they were exactly the same—all large! My heart sank, knowing that the only alternative would be to make extensive alterations to the one I had been given.

As I walked from the department, I glanced at the service desk where there was a long line of people with packages. They are like me, I thought, here trying to return or exchange Christmas presents. I stopped and stared in disbelief as a customer laid a white robe onto the counter. A white robe with pink embroidered roses, just like mine. I looked closely and saw one significant difference—it was a small size.

I listened as the customer explained to the clerk that the robe was a Christmas gift and she wanted to exchange it for a large size. I quickly pulled my robe from the bag. "You are in luck," I said to the lady, "because I have just the robe you want."

While the clerk and those around us observed the transaction, we traded robes and left the store together, both feeling we had been part of a Christmas miracle.

I have gained a few pounds since that time, but fortunately the robe is the wrap-around type. The length is perfect. The sleeves are a little short for my long arms, of course, but I don't think my daughter has ever noticed this.

My children are grown now and over the years I have received many other gifts from them, but none that was given or received with more love than the white Christmas robe.

A BLESSING ALMOST MISSED

*W*hen *my children were small, we lived in a rural area. There were no street lights or sidewalks. The nearest neighbor was about a quarter mile away. I knew the family by name only. Their house was somewhat shabby and the yard was always in need of attention. I doubted that I would have anything in common with the people who lived there. Besides, with three small children, I never seemed to have time for visiting. There was so much to do just keeping my own place neat—cutting the grass, trimming the hedge, weeding the flower beds—all of which I considered to be very important.*

One day, although I can't remember why, I visited the family down the road. I found them to be such nice people! There was even a grandmother living there, and my children quickly claimed her because their only grandparent lived hundreds of miles away. For a few months this family blessed our lives in many ways. We became close friends and had many good times together. Then they moved away, and I was left with regret that I had not gotten acquainted sooner. I can't bring back the past, but I try now to be a better neighbor, for experience has taught me that a mighty blessing may be lurking just down the street, around the corner, or at the house next door!

ENCOUNTER WITH THE SHERIFF

"Lady, tell me one more time," the sheriff said, "Just what were you and that little boy doing crawling around under that 18-wheeler?" With a pistol in his holster and handcuffs dangling at his waist, the officer stood staring into the back of the patrol car, where Maudie sat with her six–year–old son Joey.

"It's like I've been trying to tell you," Maudie said, "We were putting valve stem covers on the truck tires." From the look on his face, Maudie could tell he didn't believe her, but she continued her attempt to explain what had transpired.

"You see, officer, it all started right after we got home from church. We were a little late because Brother Sam went overtime with his sermon, which was about the importance of training up your children in the way they should go. We all changed our clothes and Joey wanted to ride his bike while I was fixing us some lunch. On Sundays we let him ride over here in this industrial park if he wants to because there isn't any traffic over here since everything is closed. He isn't allowed in the park on weekdays when the trucks are rolling—too dangerous then.

"When we bought that property across the street and built our house, all this land here in this industrial park was just open space—supposed to be tied up in some kind of ninety–nine year deal where nothing could be built on it. We hadn't been in our house more than three years before they were building all these warehouses and pretty soon trucks were running night and day—except on weekends."

"Ma'am, I really am not interested in the history of this area. If you can't explain to me why you and that little boy were under that truck with a pint jar two–thirds full of valve stem covers, I am going to have to take you both on down to headquarters," the officer warned.

Joey, with his face almost buried behind his mother's arm, began to whimper. "You are frightening this child," Maudie said, "and you should be ashamed because he is as innocent as a little lamb." Seeing the stern look on the officer's face, Maudie immediately envisioned a lamb going to slaughter and thought she had better hurry on with her explanation.

"Like I said, officer, Joey was riding his bicycle over here in the park. He came home in just a short while and was upset because he had noticed one of the tires on his bike had a valve stem cover missing. Well, his daddy told him that was all right because the cover wasn't important. To prove it was not something essential, he took one of the valve stem covers off one of our car tires and screwed it onto where one was missing on Joey's bike. Then Joey rode off again, knowing that valve stem covers are not necessary to keep the air from coming out of tires."

"Please get on with it," the officer said. Maudie wondered if he was going to give her a ticket before she had finished explaining the situation. He wasn't making it any easier for her, keeping his eyes on her and Joey like they were some kind of criminals.

"Well," Maudie said, "I was just about to finish up getting our lunch on the table when Matthew, our older son, came running into the house, yelling something about Joey and how I had better come out and see what he had done. Mercy me, I couldn't believe what I was seeing. That child had this jar over half full of valve stem covers! I asked him where they came from and he said he had taken them off of the trucks over in the industrial park because his daddy had said they were not important anyway. He thought he would take them off of the trucks and save them in case he might lose another one off of one of his bike tires sometime."

Maudie continued, "I explained to Joey that he had done a terrible thing. I said he and his brother must go and put them back onto all the valve stems on the trucks in the park. Of course, I knew he wouldn't remember exactly which ones went on which tires, but I told him they would have to just do the best they could. The problem was that Matthew said it would be a mistake for him to go with his brother because if a police car happened to come by and he and Joey were seen under the trucks, they would be accused of stealing valve stem covers, or something worse, and taken to jail. I thought he probably was right, and that is the reason I came over here with Joey, and that is why we were down there under that big truck when you yelled for us to come out and made us get into this car."

The officer finally smiled. "Lady, I believe you are telling the truth because no one could make up anything so ridiculous. Now get out of this car and see how fast you and that kid can screw on the rest of those covers." He sat in the car and watched as Maudie and Joey scurried around under those big rigs like a couple of rats until finally the jar was emptied.

The officer ordered them back to the car. Maudie was too tired and stiff to question what was going to happen next. Crawling out with difficulty, she stood and hobbled in that direction.

"Get in", he said, "and I'll drive you home." Since Maudie doubted she was able to walk even the short distance, she gladly accepted the offer. When they reached the house, the officer stepped out of the car. As he extended his hand to assist Maudie, he handed her a folded piece of paper. Dreading to see what charges were being filed against them, Maudie waited until she was inside the house before looking at the ticket she had hoped would not be issued. She stared in disbelief at the paper on which the officer had written: "It gives me pleasure to commend a mother who by example is training up her child in the way he should go."

THE WEDDING DRESS

Allison smiled at her reflection in the full–length mirror No bride ever had a more beautiful wedding dress. It was evident a lot of thought, many hours of work, and much love had gone into the creation of this magnificent gown. Small satin hearts appliquéd along the hemline of the billowing skirt were edged with thousands of tiny seed pearls. Similar hearts outlined the streamers which flowed from the saucy bow at the back of the waistband, and the veil was embellished with the most delicate of ribbon trim.

There was something else, however, that made this dress truly unique. Embroidered on the satin bodice, so as to be directly over the bride's heart, in threads of palest pink was the likeness of an angel.

Ever vivid in Allison's memory was the first time she had seen the dress. It was on her sixth birthday—the day she had been looking forward to celebrating with her friends in Miss Cooper's first grade room. Much to her dismay, she was cooped up at home with a full–blown case of chicken pox. The party had been canceled, and she was a very unhappy little girl.

It was years later that she realized her mother's decision to clean the attic that day had a purpose other than rearranging stored items and eliminating accumulated junk. To Allison the attic was a wonderland where there were dresses and hats and high–heel shoes in which she could play grown–up, and there were old trunks with scrapbooks and other treasures. Children were allowed there only in the accompaniment of an adult—a rule her father had made the day her brother fell through the ceiling and landed in the middle of the living room sofa.

Sprawled in a bean bag chair that had seen better days, Allison looked at pictures in an old album as her mother sorted through boxes and rearranged storage items. She had never before noticed the big box on the top shelf until her mother set it on the floor and unzipped the plastic covering. The pink ribbon caught her attention and she watched with interest as her mother untied the bow and lifted the top of the box.

A smile played at her mother's lips as she folded back the blue tissue paper and gently touched the dress. Though only a child, Allison had been intrigued by the beauty and softness of the fabric, the thousands of tiny seed pearls, the delicate lace, and rows of appliquéd hearts. But it was the small pink embroidered angel that had made the dress so special and had captured her heart.

The story her mother told her that day, as they sat together in the attic, had never been forgotten. Her parents, then newlyweds, had been driving from their home in Memphis to San Diego, where a new job was waiting for her father. They were young and had little of material value, but their dreams were big. They talked about the house they planned to buy when they had saved enough for a down payment and about the family they wanted to start as soon as possible.

They were deep in conversation when the station wagon sped by. The couple in front had a child between them, and through the windows her parents could see several other children bedded down in the back. On top of the station wagon were boxes and numerous pieces of luggage, partially covered by a yellow tarpaulin.

Shortly after the vehicle disappeared from their sight, her parents had rounded a sharp curve and had seen the box at the side of the road. Both had the immediate thought that it had fallen from the top of the station wagon. Stopping quickly, her father had put the box inside their car and had driven as fast as the speed limit and road conditions would allow, hoping to overtake the station wagon. His efforts were futile.

Later that night in their motel room they had opened the box, thinking they might find something to identify the owner. But there was only the beautiful wedding dress—nothing more. Knowing the owner would be distraught over the loss, they placed a notice in the local paper, giving their new California address and a phone number where they could be contacted. No response ever was received.

When they reached their new home, Allison's mother had wrapped the dress in blue tissue paper to protect the delicate fabric before sealing it in the box. It was her hope, since the owner could not be found, that some day she would have a daughter who would sense the extraordinary beauty and quality workmanship of the gown and wear it on her wedding day.

As Allison's father had advanced in his career, he was transferred to various cities across the nation. With every move, her mother made certain that the wedding dress went with them in their car. Never was it left with the packers and the moving company.

Care of the dress over the years had not been in vain, for Allison had dreamed of wearing the dress since the day her mother had folded back the blue tissue paper and told her the story of how it had been found at the side of the road.

This was the long–awaited day. Allison slowly turned in front of the mirror once more. From the tiara headpiece of gold filigree to her white embroidered slippers, she was a picture of perfection. She recalled the Old English rhyme: "Something old, something new; something borrowed, something blue." The single strand of pearls had belonged to her grandmother—something old, for continuity. The earrings, a gift from her father, were new—symbolizing optimism for the future. She had borrowed a lace handkerchief from her mother, assured that this would bring her happiness. Her garter was blue, the color for fidelity, good fortune and love.

Touching the pink angel over her heart, Allison felt both joy and sadness. She was blessed to love and be loved by such a wonderful man. Brad Harrison was honest, hard–working and handsome, fulfilling her dreams. He was one of four sons of devoted parents, and his mother had welcomed her as the daughter she never had. Yet there was sadness in her heart, knowing she was not the bride for whom the wedding dress had been fashioned. She thought of the heartbreak another bride had experienced when the loss was discovered.

True to tradition, she had not allowed Brad to see her that day—not since the evening before when he had driven her home from the rehearsal dinner. Bad luck, they had been warned, if a groom sees his bride before she walks down the aisle to become his wife. She had kept the details of her dress a secret, not even describing it to Brad or telling him how it had been found and packed away with such care by her mother.

The time had come. The wedding march resounded from the pipes of the organ, and the guests stood as she and her father walked through the doorway. She looked first into the face of Brad, and the love and adoration she saw in his eyes made her heart skip a beat. Looking to her left, she caught the reassuring smile of her mother. There was a strong bond between them, and she knew her mother was pleased with the man she had chosen as her life mate.

Hearing a faint gasp from Brad's mother as she turned in her direction, Allison noticed that her future mother–in–law was unusually pale, and her eyes were wide as though she had seen a ghost. Allison looked questionably at Brad. If he were aware of anything unusual, it did not show in his expression, and her concern waned as the ceremony began.

When the minister pronounced them husband and wife, Brad lifted his bride's veil and tenderly sealed their love with a kiss.

Before they led the recession, Brad presented a long–stemmed white rose to his newly–acquired mother–in–law, and Allison gave a like rose to Brad's mother. Leaning to plant a kiss on her cheek, Allison felt her mother–in–law's fingers tremble as she gently touched the embroidered angel on the bodice of the wedding dress.

Later, guests at the reception heard an almost unbelievable story—a story that explained the gasp that had escaped from the lips of Brad's mother when Allison and her father walked down the aisle.

Many years before, Brad's mother had worn this same wedding dress when she herself was a bride. It had been designed and made by her mother, with the lace brought from Ireland by her grandmother. Feeling that such a beautiful dress should be worn by generations of brides, his mother had stored the dress carefully, dreaming of the day she would have a daughter who also would wear it. This was not to be, for their children all were boys. She didn't discard her dream, however; she only altered it. If not a daughter, perhaps a granddaughter.

Brad was too young to remember the trip his family made to attend the wedding of his mother's sister, who had asked to borrow the wedding dress. Along with their luggage, the box with the dress had been packed on top of their station wagon. Somehow it had fallen off. His mother long ago lost hope of ever seeing the dress again.

She had nearly fainted when Allison and her father walked down the aisle. She saw the dress with the rows of appliquéd hearts, outlined with seed pearls. It was so like the dress she herself had worn more than thirty years earlier. How could this be?

When Allison leaned to kiss her, as she gave her the rose, the embroidered angel removed all doubt. The dress was back in her family. Perhaps some day her dream would become a reality, and a beautiful bride would wear her grandmother's wedding dress, uniquely adorned with a tiny pink angel.

SMILES AND HUGS

*W*hen *my younger son was in the second grade, his class visited a local nursing home. I don't know if children in public schools today have such philanthropic "field trips," but this was in 1963 and he was attending a small rural school.*

My son was a quiet, rather shy child. I wondered what his reaction to the elderly residents would be. I was confident the children would present some kind of program, and I was eager to hear all about it. When he came home from school, I began questioning him. "What kind of program did you have? Did you sing?" I shall never forget his answer. He looked up and said, "All we had to do was smile and let them hug us."

Times have changed, but human nature hasn't. Today there are many people who need a smile and a hug. They aren't all in nursing homes and hospitals, although there are many in such facilities. They are in our very midst—in our schools, in our places of employment, in our churches, in our homes.

It's a known fact—we can't run out of smiles and hugs. When we give one away, it's almost certain we will get one back!

AUNT HATTIE

Most of the folks in the little town where I have lived all my life consider Aunt Hattie to be something of a legend. During the years of my childhood and youth, I considered her to be an embarrassment.

Until her retirement three years ago, my Aunt Hattie Washburn taught the fourth grade. I dreaded moving up from the third grade, knowing I would be one of her "little ones" when the fall term began. It seems I can still hear the boys calling out, "Here comes 'Miss Hattie Washboard,'" as she ambled down the hall to the classroom. I'm sure she heard their chants, but she never let them know if it bothered her. As I think back to those days, I wonder if maybe she enjoyed the attention.

Aunt Hattie never married. She had some suitors early on, but as I heard my father say, "None of the suitors suited her." It is talked around town that Aunt Hattie is "well off," having taught school for fifty years and lived very frugally. I think she wanted to be sure none of the men got his hands on her money.

Actually "frugal" is a kind way to describe Aunt Hattie. She has always been a miser in the truest sense of the word. By definition that is one who lives miserably in order to hoard his, or her, wealth. The description fits Aunt Hattie to a T.

When I was younger, I was embarrassed by Aunt Hattie's appearance. It is not that she isn't clean, it is just the clothing she wears. Her dresses sometimes have been mended so often they look like a patchwork quilt. If she loses a button, she will replace it, but not necessarily with the same kind or color. I don't think she has ever discarded a pair of hose. They may have runs or be "near mates," but hosiery isn't a concern of Aunt Hattie, nor is the style or condition of her shoes.

While Aunt Hattie's appearance has been the source of much talk and many jokes, I don't think anyone ever criticized her as a teacher. She disciplined with a firm hand, but she taught with a loving heart. Her "little ones" soon learned she didn't have favorites and all were expected to give full attention to their studies. While most children entered her classroom reluctantly, they left in the same manner for there were few who did not grow to respect, and even love, my aunt.

As an adult, I have learned that how Aunt Hattie dresses is her own business and not a concern of mine. Now her appearance doesn't bother me, but her miserly ways do. I am her closest relative, except for two nephews whom she doesn't claim as family members because she is convinced they are just waiting for her to die in the hope of getting a nice inheritance.

Since I became Aunt Hattie's "care giver," she has undertaken to instill in me the importance of saving for the future—not just money, but every tangible thing. The old wringer washing machine on her back porch hasn't been usable for half a century, but she is sure an antique dealer will pay a big price for it someday. She hasn't done any sewing in years, but she is keeping the stacks of gingham and calico and the bolts of lace in case she should decide to make a dress or maybe an apron or two. She doesn't consider the fact that she can no longer see well enough to even thread a needle.

My first visit to Aunt Hattie's attic was a real eye–opener. I had never seen insulation in pastel shades of green and blue, interspersed with pink, yellow and white. Yet these little patches of color fill every inch between the ceiling joists. Upon closer examination, I discovered that Aunt Hattie's attic insulation is nothing more than plastic egg cartons which she has saved over the years and carefully laid side–by–side over a thin blanket of rock wool. She said it seems such a shame to throw the cartons away and the grocery will not take them back for refill.

Stacked in one corner of the attic are boxes of every size and shape. Aunt Hattie is not likely to use any of them because she is not likely to be giving presents to anyone—except on very rare occasions. She did give my son a gift when he graduated from high school, but he never cared much for monogrammed handkerchiefs, especially with the wrong initial.

I can understand saving boxes that might be used again. I do that myself. But Aunt Hattie has boxes from the days she taught school. Some have her name written on them in bold letters and are yellowed with age. The corners of others are taped together or have missing tops. I tried to make her see what a fire hazard they are, but she turned a deaf ear to my warnings. I made a mental note to see if Aunt Hattie would let me borrow a box occasionally. Maybe in a few years I will be able to at least reduce the inventory.

Aunt Hattie still drives her old 1948 Chevrolet, although she doesn't go farther than the beauty shop. She gets her hair trimmed about every six weeks and twice a year she goes for a permanent wave. She always shampoos her hair at home. She claims leaning back onto the shampoo bowl hurts her neck, but the real reason is that the operator, after much urging, agreed to give her a one dollar discount.

There are two big grocery stores in our town now. Aunt Hattie clips coupons and studies the weekly ads for the lowest prices, going from one store to the other for the best bargains. She had a recent experience that I found disgraceful, but she related it to me with absolute delight.

As she cruised the aisles with an empty cart, looking for an advertised special on bread at one of the stores, she nearly collided with another shopper whose basket was quite full. The lady spoke kindly to Aunt Hattie and asked if she was finding everything she needed. Aunt Hattie said, "No, but you must be, from the looks of your basket." They met again on the next aisle, the lady noticing Aunt Hattie's still empty basket and, no doubt, her deceiving appearance. As they came toward each other for the third time, the lady reached out and touched Aunt Hattie's arm.

"Would you mind," she asked, "if I gave you something?" It is evident she didn't know my Aunt Hattie or she would have known this little lady never turned down a gift of any kind. Aunt Hattie just sort of smiled and tucked her head as the lady thrust two crumpled $20 bills into her hand.

She could hardly wait to tell me about her good fortune.

In all likelihood my aunt will not live to spend all her money, yet she continues to live like a pauper. "Waste not, want not" is more than just a slogan to Aunt Hattie, but I did not realize the full extent of her frugality until I recently found a box in her storage cabinet. I smiled as I read the label: "String that is too short to be of any use."

She is becoming rather frail now and says she is looking forward to getting her angel wings. I'll miss her when that day comes, but I know my Aunt Hattie. She'll be up there flying around, looking for that pot of gold at the end of the rainbow.

THE PREACHER WORE TENNIS SHOES

*I*t was laity Sunday. The theme of our morning
worship service was Stewardship. The lay leader
spoke on "The High Cost of Becoming Involved."
The choir sang "Give of Your Best to the Master." To
close the service, the Youth Department presented an
original skit in which all members of a family pledged
to become actively involved in the ministry of their
church. Each of them recruited others to help, thereby
not only sharing the workload, but also sharing the joy
that comes from being a good steward.

Although the emphasis of the skit was on laity—men,
women, youth and children—the script included
enlisting the participation of the minister, whose role
also was played by one of the youth. At the appointed
time, he rose from his seat in the congregation and
walked down the aisle in his ministerial robe. Facing
the young man from her seat next to me in the choir
loft, his mother gasped, "The preacher is wearing
tennis shoes!"

Yes, the preacher certainly was wearing tennis
shoes—big, white, size 12 tennis shoes. They glared
from beneath a robe that was approximately 18 inches
above his ankles.

"The preacher is wearing tennis shoes." The statement kept going through my mind. I could see that the tennis shoes were quite appropriate, for those wearing such most often have busy feet, and whose feet are busier than those of a preacher! Those men and women who have answered God's call are seldom idle. They go from their churches to the hospitals, to comfort the sick and bereaved, to call on shut–ins, to visit prospective members, to attend committee meetings, sessions of the administrative board, and the council on ministries. The list goes on and on. They must continue their education, attend pastors' school, and participate in retreats. Somewhere in between all this, and much more, they must find time to prepare their sermons. Yes, preachers surely need to wear tennis shoes.

I had another thought. What about the laity? Maybe everyone needs tennis shoes. Sunday School classes for all ages need dedicated teachers. The youth need counselors. The choir could use more members. Leadership is needed in the Scout and sports programs. The women's study group and men's organization seek the involvement of every church member.

I realized I should consider my own shoes. Are the heels so high that I see over all the areas of need? Are my shoes new and pinching my toes, not comfortable enough for work that needs to be done? Maybe my shoes have broken strings that need to be replaced.

As the youthful preacher gave the benediction, I added my own prayer—that I might always wear the shoes of a good steward.

LULA BETTERBEE'S CHRISTMAS TREE

Having joined the staff of *The Star Gazette* only two weeks earlier, I was excited when the editor himself called me into his office. "Annie," he said, "I think this is a story right down your alley. Check out this old lady and see if she is as eccentric as her neighbors claim."

I was uncertain whether I should feel complimented or insulted to be given this assignment. I was pleased that he had remembered my name, but he had said this story should be "right down my alley." Was he implying that I, too, was an eccentric old lady?

I muttered a weak, "Thank you, Mr. Pauley. I'll get right on it." I grabbed a city map, along with my note pad, camera and purse, and was on my way.

Mr. Pauley, a man of few words, had not given me much information. He said he had been getting calls from the lady's neighbors, complaining about her Christmas decorations and her nightly ritual of burning sparklers in her front yard. She had discontinued the fireworks after the second visit by the police, who had warned that they would be taking her in if she shot off another skyrocket. Still the neighbors complained that her behavior was degrading to their cove.

As I left the parking lot, I glanced again at the slip of paper Mr. Pauley had given me. All that was written on it was "Mrs. Lula Betterbee, 1805 Muy Bonita Cove." I had never been in that part of the city. It was what was referred to as "Out East"—certainly out of my modest neighborhood.

From my high school Spanish, I knew that "Muy Bonita" meant "very pretty," and the name certainly was appropriate. I gasped when I turned into the cove. All the houses seemed to be nestled in a pink and white forest with dogwood and redbud trees in full bloom. Azaleas—white, pink and shades of lavender— turned the entire cove into a fairyland. Lawns were perfectly manicured. The beauty of it all left no doubt that the people who lived on Muy Bonita Cove took great pride in their property.

It was not difficult to spot Number 1805. It was not that Mrs. Betterbee's lawn and spring flowers and trees were not as beautiful as those of her neighbors. It was the Christmas tree in her front window that attracted immediate attention. With its blinking red and green lights and the shining star at the top, it definitely seemed out of place for the middle of April. The snowman wreath on the front door added to my nervousness as I rang the bell.

Mrs. Betterbee wasn't at all as I had pictured her in my mind. She was such a petite lady. Her once blonde hair, now almost white, framed her cherub–like face in soft curls. When I introduced myself, her eyes sparkled like the glitter on the pot of silk poinsettia that centered her hall table. She invited me inside, giving me a warm smile and a gentle pat on my arm.

"Oh," she said, "I know why you are here. You want to see my tree. Some of my neighbors think I'm a bit daffy. They are always complaining to the police or the mayor. I guess now they have called your paper, but I don't pay them any mind. Of course I did have to stop the fireworks, and they were so pretty. But the police said there is some kind of law against shooting off fireworks inside the city. I was always very careful with them, but the officers were not very understanding."

I stepped into the "front room" as she called it, and there stood the tree in all its glory. Underneath it were beautifully wrapped packages. Every nook and cranny of the room had been decorated as if Mrs. Betterbee might be expecting Santa Claus that very night. She flipped on the stereo and Christmas carols added the final touch to the holiday setting.

After the shock of it all began to wear off a bit, I remembered why I was there. "Is there a special reason you celebrate Christmas in mid–April?" I asked.

Mrs. Betterbee chuckled and said, "Oh, I celebrate Christmas all year long. This beautiful tree has been right here for more than five years."

She remembered it all so well. Bob and Janet were such a nice young couple. She had been their real estate agent and had sold them their first house. They had wanted to get moved in before Christmas, but the seller had some health problems and the closing was postponed several times.

It wasn't easy to get all the papers signed, but she had used her feminine charms and somehow she pulled it all together. They were settled in a week before Christmas and Mrs. Betterbee had stopped by with a little housewarming gift. She had admired their tree, lamenting that she had been too busy to get hers down from the attic. Since her children were busy with their own families and wouldn't be coming home that year, it was all right. She probably would just sort of skip Christmas for once in her life.

It was early Christmas Eve. She had answered the knock at her door and there they stood. "Where's your old plastic tree?" Bob had asked with a grin. "I'll set it up, and Janet can start decorating it while I go to the store for some steaks."

It had been such a wonderful evening. Now the tree and all the decorations served as reminders of that night and the kindness of the young couple who didn't want Christmas to bypass the realtor who had been relentless in her efforts to see that they would be able to spend Christmas in their new home.

Mrs. Betterbee turned to me with a smile. "I never use this room anyway except during the holidays. It would be a shame to take down the tree and pack it away for a year. Besides, I don't have a very good working relationship with Christmas trees."

She explained that her late husband had always set up their tree and circled it with strings of lights. Her only contribution was adding the many ornaments which they had collected during their travels. That first Christmas after he died, she had dragged the tree down from the attic and set it up herself. It had been a much harder job than she had anticipated, but when she lay back on the sofa at 2:00 a.m. to admire the finished product, she felt good. And tired! Two hours later she awoke with a start. There was her tree lying flat in the middle of the floor. She covered it with a sheet, pronounced it dead, and went to bed.

The memory of that experience had influenced her decision to leave the present tree in the front room, not to be taken down and carried to the attic year after year. She admitted, though, that this past Christmas she'd had a hankering for a second tree, a white flocked one for the den. She had bought a beautiful spruce and several cans of spray–on flocking. The weather was not cooperative. It was the day after Christmas when the rain finally ended. Not to be defeated, she had taken the tree out to her front yard and had given it a good flocking before putting it at curbside for garbage pickup.

Mrs. Betterbee's neighbors may think she is a bit strange, and maybe she is. But I like her. She has a great attitude, a lot of fortitude, and a marvelous sense of humor. What's more, she keeps the Christmas spirit alive all year—not only in her heart, but also in her front room.

CAKE ICER

*F*illing out the census form was a snap for most of our friends and relatives; they received the short form. We received one of the long forms, with page after page of questions. The multiple–choice questions were the most difficult because there wasn't always an appropriate answer to select. "Spouse's occupation" presented a problem for us. There was no choice that even remotely fit the work that I was doing at that time, although some unusual occupations were listed. The one we found most amusing was "Cake Icer." This seemed a rather odd occupation to be included on the census form.

Recently we had a dinner and evening of entertainment at our church to benefit a special mission project. I invited Judy, a much–loved former member, to attend. Having moved more than 100 miles away, she had not been back to visit in several years. What a joy it was to see her! What a pleasure it was to watch other church members greet her with smiles and hugs as they reminisced about days gone by and experiences that they had shared.

The evening was a great success. Both the dinner and program were good. The crowd was enthusiastic, *and the mission project was boosted by more than $500. But having Judy with us was extra special. She was "the frosting on the cake." Then the thought hit me—Judy is a "cake icer."*

The census bureau may think a cake icer is someone who works in a bakery, but that is not necessarily true. My friend Judy is a "cake icer" and she works for a utility company. Perhaps this should be a challenge for all of us—to so live that one day we can truthfully list our occupation as "cake icer."

THE TREASURE CHEST

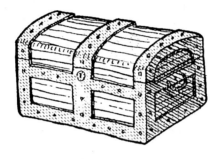

School was still out for the Christmas holidays. When I answered the knock at my front door, there stood my little neighbor, Jennifer, and her two visiting cousins from Ohio, Joanna and Amanda. Earlier I had watched them playing in the cove and had remarked to my husband that little Jennifer, a dimpled blue–eyed blonde, was such a contrast to her cousins, who had shiny black hair and big brown eyes.

My husband and I have no children of our own, but we became Aunt Rubye and Uncle Charlie to Jennifer soon after her family moved into the house next door.

Jennifer, who had just turned seven and was in the second grade, had taught me a lot of things, like how to play Old Maid and Go Fishing. And I had never had trouble finding a helper when baking cookies or making popcorn balls.

"Please, Aunt Rubye," she said when I opened the door, "will you open your treasure chest and let my cousins see Sarah Jane?"

First, I should explain that I really don't have a treasure chest. It's just a small, very old trunk in which I keep "Sarah Jane" and some other things that have little or no real value, but hold too many memories for me to throw them away.

I invited my young guests in and we went to the back bedroom to open the "treasure chest."

Jennifer reached down and lovingly patted Sarah Jane and, with great importance, explained to Amanda and Joanna that Aunt Rubye had had this doll for a long, long time—since she was seven years old herself. Jennifer's cousins seemed mightily impressed, looking from the doll to me, as if to say, "Can the doll really be THAT old?"

"Is she more than fifty years old?" asked Joanna.

"Oh, yes," I said with a smile. They listened attentively as I told them how I came to get Sarah Jane.

My family were sharecroppers, and we lived in a rural area of Arkansas. I explained to my little friends about sharecroppers, who are just what the name implies. They live on someone else's farm and "share the crop." I was a child during the Great Depression of the 1930s, and my family's share was a place to live and, most of the time, enough food for our table. When crops are not good, sharecroppers often move. We moved a lot. I was happy if I got to stay in one school the entire year.

I started the second grade at Oak Hill School, which was just a one-room school. There were about thirty children, ranging from the first through the eighth grades, all taught by Mr. Miller. Only later did I realize what a wonderful, dedicated teacher he was, coming to school early to make a fire in that old potbellied stove during winter months when few, if any, of us had clothes warm enough or shoes without holes in the soles.

I don't recall that discipline was ever a problem because most of us were eager to learn. It was exciting to hear about faraway countries and read those wonderful books in Mr. Miller's cabinet. Sometimes he would let us take a book home to share with our parents.

And what fun I had at recess! At home there was no one for me to play with except for my three–year–old sister, but at school there were other children. Best of all, there was Jesse. Jesse Cline was my idol. His hair was cropped short all around, but it fell on his forehead in a mass of blond curls.

No one ever had a crush like I had on Jesse. I was sure we would grow up and marry and live happily ever after. Actually, I don't think Jesse was aware of my affection. I was new in that school and very shy. I didn't yet have any close friends, so I kept my secret love for Jesse all to myself. One day, though, I did hit him with a snowball. I thought that should let him know that I really liked him a lot.

Christmas was approaching, and Mr. Miller had us all draw names. I was so excited when I found out that Jesse had drawn my name. I knew without a shadow of a doubt that I would get something real nice from Jesse. My daddy and mother had already explained to me that all those wonderful toys in the Sears, Roebuck catalog had been promised to other children and that Santa Claus would never be able to get all the way out to our house.

I had looked under the bed, though, and found a corn shuck doll that my mother had made for me and what looked like a doll bed that I thought my daddy had made. We would go to the church on Christmas

Eve, and all us children would get an apple and an orange, some raisins, and maybe a candy cane. What I wanted more than anything, though, was a real doll—a real store–bought doll. "Someday, Rubye, someday. You just wait. Someday you will have your doll," my mother said. I knew "someday" wasn't going to be anytime soon.

It really didn't matter so much that I wouldn't be getting a real doll for Christmas because Jesse had drawn my name. I knew I wouldn't get a doll from him, but maybe a box of crayons. Could it be that he might even give me some cutout paper dolls like I had seen in Mr. Murphy's store? Every night I dreamed about what my present might be.

The big boys at school had cut down a cedar tree and made a stand for it. With the skimpy side turned to the wall, it looked just wonderful in the corner farthest from the stove. We had decorated it with strings of popcorn and red berries and paper chains. One of the big girls had even made a bright star for the very top of the tree. I thought it must be the most beautiful Christmas tree in the whole wide world.

Mr. Miller had said we could bring our present for the person whose name we had drawn any day during the week before the Christmas holidays. By the middle of the week, there were a lot of presents under the tree. I watched every morning to see what Jesse would bring, but he seemed to always come in empty–handed. I was sure he had slipped something in when I wasn't looking so he could surprise me. I could hardly wait until the gifts would be given out.

Finally the day came. Mr. Miller read Christmas stories to us and we played some games and sang carols. I was so excited. Even my biscuit and fried egg lunch tasted better than usual.

At last it was time! Mr. Miller read the name on each present, and the children went up, one by one, to get their gifts. That is, everyone went but me.

Mr. Miller surely did not realize he had not called my name—that there was no present under the tree for me.

School was dismissed and the other children ran out with shouts of "Merry Christmas" and "Happy New Year." I hurried out too, but I didn't run with the others. I hid behind the schoolhouse until everyone had gone. I didn't want anyone to see me crying. My heart was broken. I could not believe Jesse had not brought a present for me. He had run out of the schoolhouse, right by me, without a word. How could he be so mean?

My mother didn't know what was wrong, but one look at my tear–stained face and red eyes and she just threw open her arms. Between sobs, I told her what had happened. Nothing could be worse than being the only one in school without a present under the tree, especially knowing it was Jesse who had drawn my name. He hadn't brought me anything at all, and I had loved him so much, even if no one but me knew it.

Mama didn't have an answer, only loving arms that held me close until my tears stopped.

I wasn't hungry at supper that night. Daddy tried to cheer me. He talked about the Christmas program at church and what fun we would have together with our neighbors, but it didn't seem important to me anymore.

Mama was baking cookies when I got up the next morning. Usually I was right there to help roll out the dough, but even that didn't hold any interest for me. All I could think about was Jesse, who had betrayed me.

We were just finishing supper that night when there was a knock at our door. We didn't have many visitors, especially at night. Daddy went to the door and then he called me.

There stood Mr. Cline, Jesse's father, with a sack in his hand. As he handed it to me, he leaned down and hugged me real tight. "Rubye," he said, "this is from Jesse. He wanted to put it under the tree at school, but there just was no money to buy anything for you until I got paid today. I'm sorry your present is late."

Mr. Cline came in to get warm before he walked the eight miles back to his house. He watched with Mama and Daddy as I opened the sack. There was my first real, store–bought doll, with golden hair and eyes that opened and closed. My dream come true! My Sarah Jane. Never had I been so happy.

When Jesse's father had gone, I heard Daddy and Mama talking about Mr. Cline's coming in the cold to bring me such an expensive gift. The Clines were sharecroppers too. Besides Jesse, there were several other children in the family. None of them was likely to get anything for Christmas as nice as my doll.

Perhaps Jennifer was right in calling my old trunk a treasure chest, for surely the doll it holds is a true treasure. It mended the broken heart of a little girl. More than that, over the years Sarah Jane has been a reminder of the true spirit of Christmas, that of love and sacrifice. The spirit that puts a song in our hearts and causes us to sing with gladness, "Joy to the world, the Lord has come."

MEMORIES
(Of a Caribbean Cruise)

Memories of salty spray,
Cool upon my face,
Riding Caribbean waves
In a carefree chase.
Memories of mornings–
Alone, just God and me,
In quietness to behold
The beauty of the sea.
Memories of laughter
Such tales as were spun!
Stories of the mariners,
Hours shared in fun.
Memories of islands–
The glory they contain,
Every leaf set sparkling
By refreshing rain.

Memories of people–
Beggars on the street,
Martinique folk dancers–
The rhythm of their feet.
Memories of churches–
Built with loving care;
Hearts bowed in worship,
Knowing God is there.
Memories of friendships–
Kindled while at sea;
Strangers before sailing,
Now endeared to me.
These memories are mine,
Of the islands and the sea.
Time cannot erase them;
They are a part of me.

THE HITCHHIKERS

"Hitching to Florida will be a cinch," Jim Bob told his friend Tony as he showed him the map on which he had drawn a line from Memphis to the Florida coast. "Two good looking boys like us shouldn't have any trouble," he continued, "and if we don't go now, we may never have another chance." They would be graduating in the spring and that meant full–time jobs unless they enrolled in the local college, which wasn't likely.

Their hitchhiking experience was limited to catching a ride to the ball field or to school when they missed the bus, but Jim Bob had dreamed of going to Florida since he was in the fourth grade. That was when Margaret Ann Blake, the girl he was secretly in love with, had reported to the class that her family had gone to Florida on summer vacation. She not only had seen the ocean, but she had made sand castles on the beach and she had a quart jar filled with shells she and her sister had collected.

That was the first time Jim Bob had heard of anyone going on a vacation trip. Certainly not him or any of the families who lived in his neighborhood. The Blakes lived on the other side of the railroad, and Margaret Ann's father usually drove her to school in their station wagon. Jim Bob's family didn't own a car, and the only trip he had ever taken was on a bus to visit his grandparents on their North Mississippi farm. He didn't consider that a pleasure trip because he usually got "bus sick" and besides, he didn't believe people actually enjoyed feeding pigs and milking cows. He preferred the city, with such conveniences as indoor plumbing.

Talking Tony into going to Florida was no problem. Although they were in the same grade, Jim Bob was nearly a year older because he didn't start first grade until he was almost seven. Anything Tony wanted to know, all he had to do was ask Jim Bob. He knew everything—or at least so Tony thought. He never questioned the accuracy of the information. The difficulty would be getting away for a few days. Jim Bob had that figured out, though. He would tell his parents he would be staying with Tony, which he sometimes did, and Tony would say he was going to spend a couple nights with Jim Bob. Neither would be exactly lying because they would be staying together—in Florida!

"We should leave early Friday morning," Jim Bob said, "and that way we will get to Florida before sundown. We can enjoy two full days on the beach and be back home before Monday night." It sounded good to Tony.

Only essentials were packed into their shared canvas bag. Tooth brushes, combs, clean underwear, a change of shirts and two towels (for the beach). "We don't want to take too much with us," Jim Bob said, "because there might not be much room in the cars that will be stopping to give us a ride." He tucked the well–worn map into the hip pocket of his cut–off jeans as they headed for Highway 78, which Jim Bob figured would be the fastest and most direct route to the wondrous state of Florida.

A few cars passed them by, but the boys figured that was because there wasn't room for the two of them. Before they had time to doubt their ability to get a ride, a truck stopped. Hitched to it was a flatbed trailer loaded with household furnishings. "Boys," the driver said, "you can ride up front here with me or you can sit back there on that sofa." They chose the sofa and waved to everyone they passed. The trip was going great—for about ten miles.

"End of the line," the man called as he stopped to let them climb down before he turned onto a side road.

Their next ride was with an "elderly" couple. Jim Bob whispered to Tony that he hoped the man could still see well enough to drive all right. "I bet he is at least 60 years old," Jim Bob said. "He looks about the same age as my grandfather." There was no problem with the man's driving; it was the lady's questioning that made them nervous. She thought they had run away from home and wanted to know what they had done that made them decide to leave. Neither of them minded that this too was a short ride.

Over the next few hours they were in and out of a half dozen cars and a couple of pickup trucks, none of which was going many miles in the direction of Florida. It was encouraging, however, that so many people stopped for them. That is, they stopped until late afternoon. As darkness fell, there was less traffic and cars seemed to be going much faster as they passed.

"I guess they can't see us very well in the dark," Jim Bob said, "but I'm sure someone will pick us up in the morning." He didn't want Tony to become discouraged, even though he himself was getting tired of walking. About midnight they spread their towels on the ground behind a billboard and both slept until the sun in their faces awakened them.

With aching backs and empty stomachs, they headed for a small grocery store in the distance. After washing their faces at the outside hydrant, each decided on a Moon Pie and R. C. Cola for breakfast.

"At home I would be having scrambled eggs with hot biscuits and gravy," Tony said, as he licked the last crumbs from his fingers.

"Me, too. But just wait until we get to Florida and we'll have fresh oranges every morning—probably pick all we want right off the trees," Jim Bob said with a grin.

Early morning traffic passed the boys as if they were invisible. "Probably trying to get to work on time," Jim Bob said, forgetting that it was Saturday and most business offices were closed. They walked until nearly noon, their thumbs getting no results. In fact, everyone seemed to speed up and move to the other side of the road when approaching them.

"What's wrong?" Tony questioned. But even Jim Bob, who knew everything, was puzzled.

At a service station, where the boys stopped for a drink of water, they heard shocking news. A motorist had been killed and his car stolen by a young hitchhiker. After crashing into a utility pole, the murderer had abandoned the car and was last seen running along the highway, his thumb in the air.

By late afternoon, having walked all day with no one stopping, the boys realized the prospect of their getting to Florida was bleak. "If I was at home, I'd be having pork chops and mashed potatoes tonight," Tony lamented. That gave Jim Bob an idea.

"You go over to the other side of the highway, Tony, and thumb back toward Memphis, and I will keep trying to get someone to stop who is headed south. If someone stops for you, I'll come running over there; if a car stops for me, I'll ask 'em to wait for you," Jim Bob said, "and we'll just go whichever way we can get a ride." No one stopped going either direction.

By morning desperation was setting in. Hearing a train in the distance gave Jim Bob another brainstorm. The railroad track ran parallel to the highway. They would hop the next freight train headed in the direction of Memphis. They were in luck, reaching the track just as the train slowed in its approach to what they figured to be a town in South Georgia. When the train came to a complete stop, they were able to climb into an open-top gondola car. Soon the train was moving and as it picked up speed, both felt confident they would be sleeping in their own beds that night.

Although disappointed that they never got to Florida, they consoled themselves with the thought of telling their friends about their adventure. No one they knew had ever hopped a train. It was a great way to travel—until they went through a tunnel. Cinders and smoke from the coal-burning engine nearly smothered them as they lay on the floor of the gondola, struggling to breathe. Subsequent tunnels brought more of the same, but there was no way to escape as the train speeded on. Hours later the train slowed when approaching Birmingham. The boys jumped and ran, fearing they would be arrested if caught.

For once, Jim Bob's freckles were not visible. His face, hair, body and clothes, like those of Tony, were covered in a layer of black soot. They were dirty, tired and hungry as they made their way to a house a short distance from where they had jumped. A grandmotherly–looking lady who took pity on them answered their knock at the door. In spite of their condition, she invited them into her kitchen and watched in amazement at the amount of food two hungry boys could devour.

Feeling better after having eaten their first real food in two days, the boys thanked the lady and set out walking once again. Spotting a barbershop on the outskirts of the city, they spent the last of their money there, taking a shower and changing into their clean clothes. It was here their luck changed. A northbound trucker, himself the father of four sons, offered them a ride all the way to Memphis. There was no hesitation in their acceptance. They had to walk only about half a mile from where the trucker bade them farewell.

Neither was bothered that they never got to Florida. After all, building sand castles and collecting shells surely wasn't as exciting as thumbing rides, hopping a freight train, begging breakfast like a real hobo, showering at a barber shop and completing their adventure in the cab of a shiny 18-wheeler. Moreover, two young hitchhikers now knew the truth of the statement: "There's no place like home."

THE FLIGHT HOME

T rudging along toward Gate 36 with a bag of San Francisco sourdough bread in one hand, attaché case in the other, and raincoat over my arm, I wondered why my flight always seemed to depart from the farthest gate. I was in pain. My head ached. My feet ached. Parts in between felt like I had been hit by a runaway cable car.

San Francisco is a wonderful city, but a four–day convention there can do terrible things to one's body. I was ready for Memphis and a quiet weekend at home.

It is my policy never to fly on a Friday afternoon unless absolutely necessary. But this was a necessity. If I didn't make this flight it would mean a cab back to the hotel and another night away from my family. I could see a crowd milling around at the distant gate. I was sure the flight would be full, if not over–booked. I wouldn't volunteer to give up my seat if they offered a free round-trip ticket to Paris. All I wanted to do was board the plane, get settled into my reserved aisle seat, and sleep all the way home. I was considering faking a sprained ankle so I could get early boarding privilege with those needing assistance or a little extra time. However, by the time I reached the gate, boarding by rows had begun.

I eased into the long line and gave a sigh of relief that I was about to board. I tried to return the flight attendant's cheerful greeting, but my forced smile lasted only a minute. In my aisle seat was an elderly lady, buckled in and settled down for the flight. I suggested that she move over next to the window, explaining that she was in my seat.

"No," she said, "This is where they told me to sit."

She had no intention of moving, and I had no intention of taking the window seat. I like an aisle seat and this was the one I had reserved. I bucked the oncoming passengers to solicit help from the flight attendant, whose smile was beginning to fade.

It was with great reluctance that the old lady finally moved. The flight attendant had explained that she could now look out the window. That was not a good selling point. She did not want to look out. She was sure if she was looking out when we took off, she would get air sick. She wanted me to let her know when we were in the air. I promised I would.

I closed my eyes, hoping for peace and quiet. Not to be had. The little lady proceeded to inform me that she had gone to California on a bus to visit her son. Just a few days before she was to return home, she had twisted her ankle. The doctor had said she should keep it elevated as much as possible to prevent swelling. Realizing it now would not be advisable for her to spend several days on the bus, her son had purchased the plane ticket. This was the first time she had ever flown. This I believed to be true.

In my semi–conscious state, I later realized that we were still on the ground. I managed to focus my eyes on my faithful Timex and could see we should have been well on our way. The flight attendant soon was passing down the aisle, explaining our delay. Of course I had to repeat her message to the old lady beside me.

"One of the toilets is out of order," I said, "and since the plane is fully loaded and the flight will be several hours, they want to repair it before we take off."

She shrugged her shoulders and said, "Well, I wasn't planning to use the toilet before we get to Memphis anyway." I could see smiles on faces of passengers to the front, rear and side of us. The fun had only just begun!

Faithful to my promise, I informed the little lady when at last we were airborne.

"Are we going to have a movie now?" she asked.

"No, ma'am. Movies are shown only on the big planes," I said. I could see the disappointment on her face as she looked at me in total bewilderment.

"But isn't this a big plane?" she asked.

I reminded myself that this was her first flight. Moreover, I had been taught to respect my elders. I pointed out, with what patience I could muster, that the plane was small compared to the jumbo jets, and it did not have a screen on which movies could be shown.

I was saved from further discussion of in–flight movies with the arrival of the flight attendant, once again smiling as she pushed the drink cart. A cup of black coffee was just what I needed. The little lady was adamant that she wanted nothing.

"Maybe you would like a glass of juice," I suggested. Looking me right in the eye, she told me in no uncertain terms that she did not want juice or anything else. I smiled to myself, recalling that she had said she didn't plan to use the restroom until we got to Memphis. I figured she had decided against any liquid intake.

It was not until the passengers several rows ahead had been served that she turned to me and asked what would be the cost of a glass of orange juice. She looked at me in such a child-like manner that the wall I had tried to put between us began to crumble. I explained that beverages were complimentary and called to the flight attendant that my friend in the window seat would like some orange juice.

She fumbled with her seat belt and asked for my assistance in unbuckling it. I must have been mistaken about the restroom matter. But no, she didn't want to go anywhere. She just didn't want the seat belt fastened. I explained the airline policy that all passengers are asked to keep their seat belts fastened as a safety precaution in the event turbulent weather should be experienced. She looked at me and then at several passengers moving down the aisle toward the rear of the plane.

"Where are those people going?" she asked.

"Probably to the restroom," I replied, wondering why she couldn't figure that out herself.

"Well," she said very matter-of-factly, "I guess they must have their seat belts unfastened." I leaned over and released the buckle on her seat belt.

Choosing which entree she would have at mealtime was a big decision. Her son had explained to her that the meal was included in the price of the ticket even though he had failed to tell her about the complimentary beverages. Now she wanted my opinion. Should she have the baked chicken or the lasagna? She didn't want anything that might upset her stomach. I agreed with her on that! I suggested the chicken— for both of us. Personally, I preferred lasagna. But I had a feeling if I got lasagna, she would decide my meal looked better than hers and would want me to summon the flight attendant and get her meal changed.

Chicken was a good choice. She had no complaints about the meal. The trays were removed. It was nap time. I had hardly closed my eyes before I felt her tugging at my sleeve. "Why are we flying along the highway?" she asked as she pointed out the window.

At 35,000 feet, above a layer of clouds, I knew there was no possible way she could be seeing the highway. At her insistence, I leaned over to look. I'm not sure that I ever really convinced her what she was seeing was the wing of our plane.

Finally she dozed off. No more than ten minutes later, she was awake and ready for more conversation. I was informed that she lived in Arkansas, but she had to fly to Memphis because that was the nearest airport. Her son had arranged for one of her neighbors to meet her when she arrived, and this nice man would drive her to her home in Marion, Arkansas.

I welcomed the announcement that we were in the approach pattern for the Memphis International Airport; albeit the flight certainly had not been boring. The flight attendant suddenly appeared, holding forth a bottle of champagne toward my seat companion. "For you," she said to the lady, "to celebrate your first plane ride."

My friend, as I now had come to consider her, looked to me for an explanation. "It's a bottle of champagne, a gift from the airline, so you will remember your first flight."

Her comment was emphatic. "I don't drink."

Now it was the flight attendant's turn to be baffled. She was not accustomed to anyone turning down a bottle of champagne. I suggested to my traveling companion that she reconsider. Surely she must know someone whom she could give it to. She reckoned her neighbor who was meeting her in

Memphis would appreciate it. So it was settled. She accepted the gift, although rather reluctantly.

As soon as we had landed and the seat belt sign was turned off, she was standing, ready to deplane. Leaning impatiently on the back of the seat in front of her and looking over the shoulder of the gentleman still seated there, she declared loud enough to be heard by those in the rear of the plane, "This man just had his first flight, too."

I could feel eyes turning our way as I asked how she came by this information. "Because he's got a bottle of champagne too," she informed me, as well as all the other passengers within earshot.

This was too much. I peered over the seat to see that bottle of champagne for myself. The man whose ears now were turning from pink to red did not have a bottle of champagne. What he had was a folding umbrella, with the handle upturned.

The passengers had begun to move forward. I stepped into the aisle and made room ahead of me for the little lady, clutching her bottle of champagne. I knew why the other passengers were smiling. At least they had enjoyed in–flight entertainment.

The entire crew was lined up at the front of the plane. As I approached the door, one of the flight attendants reached out to present me with a bottle of champagne.

"This one is for you, with our appreciation. You deserve it."

Unlike the lady from Arkansas, I readily accepted the gift.

THE GIRL
WHO COULDN'T SING

"I'm Little Red Riding Hood, trying to be so good..."
Annie softly sang as she waited for her students to assemble in the music room at the new school where she was beginning her career as a fourth-grade teacher. Her thoughts went back to the time when she herself was in the fourth grade. How different her school was from this one with computers in every classroom and the availability of the latest technology!

Annie's childhood was spent on a small farm. Born during the Great Depression, she was the youngest of eight children, the oldest being her sister Alice. Twenty-one years and six boys later, Annie joined the family. Like all her siblings, she had attended the small elementary school about three miles from their home. Two grades were combined in each of the four classrooms. After finishing the eighth grade there, she rode the big yellow bus to the high school in the neighboring town. Although the total number of children in the four-room school she had attended was less than in the combined fourth grade classes where she now taught, Annie felt her early education had not been lacking in any way. The teachers knew the families of their students, and most parents eagerly participated in activities at the school.

While she had many happy memories of her early school days, there had been one disappointing aspect. Every spring the school presented an operetta to which the entire community was invited. Miss Craig, who taught first and second grades, was in charge of the school's music program and had the responsibility for the annual production. It was only natural that the leading parts were assigned to those with the best voices. Annie always was a flower in the garden or a tree in the forest—a part that did not require her to sing except as one of a large group. She still remembered the day she overheard Miss Craig say to one of the other teachers, "Annie could not carry a tune in a 10–gallon bucket."

She was in the fourth grade when "Little Red Riding Hood" was announced as the operetta that would be performed by the students that year. Annie so wanted to wear the little red cape—to carry the basket of goodies to Grandmother. But she didn't get the part. It went to her friend Martha Louise, who was a year younger. As they played together at recess, Martha Louise practiced the songs she would sing. Soon Annie knew all the words, but the tunes remained a problem. "I can't understand," she tearfully complained to her mother, "why the music in my head won't come out of my mouth like I want it to." No matter how hard she tried to sing like Martha Louise, her efforts were in vain.

The week before the operetta was to be performed, Martha Louise became ill and was unable to attend school.

Much to Miss Craig's dismay, Annie was the only one who knew all the songs that Little Red Riding Hood was to sing; moreover the pretty red hooded cape fit her perfectly. Although sorry her friend was ill, Annie could not believe her own good fortune. She desperately tried to get the tunes right, but she could see the disappointment on Miss Craig's face as she told her to "go home and practice more." Annie did. She sang to the chickens and cows and pigs. She sang in the house and in the garden. She sang alone under a big tree in the meadow, pretending she was on the stage at her school. It was the day before the operetta when her world fell apart. Martha Louise made a miraculous recovery, reclaimed her red hooded cape, and sang her way "through the woods to Grandmother's house" while Annie once again became a flower by the side of the path.

The following year was equally disappointing. "Peter Rabbit" was Miss Craig's chosen operetta. Robert had the leading part, which Annie thought was grand since she was secretly in love with him. She just wanted to be a head of lettuce in Mr. McGregor's garden. Those costumes were made of layers upon layers of pale green crepe paper, cut and put together to resemble lettuce leaves, and there were little hats made of the same paper. There were only four heads of lettuce so each child needed to have a good voice. Annie knew the lettuce song, word for word, but Miss Craig picked her to be a carrot. There was a long row of carrots, and they sang very little.

She could still remember exactly what they sang: *"We are the carrots, bonnie little carrots, living in McGregor's garden. Slender and snappy, very, very happy, living here to ripen and harden. Then along comes a rabbit, with a naughty little habit, and nibbles, nibbles, nibbles us away."* Then they did a toe–to–heel dance, which Annie thought was rather silly. Besides that, the costumes were tacky—just two big carrots cut out of orange cardboard and fastened together with straps over the shoulders, so that one carrot hung in front and one in back. Carrots could not even sit!

When Annie was in the sixth grade, she was selected to represent the school as a princess for the Crown and Scepter Ball, one of the special events of the annual Memphis Cotton Carnival. Every school in the city and county contributed to the King and Queen's Royal Court by providing a prince, princess and two pages. No singing involved! Annie remembered this as one of the highlights of her school days. In her photo album she had pictures of herself and Prince Timothy and their pages. Her dress had a silver bodice, and silver stars danced over the royal blue skirt, made of six layers of stiff, net–like material. A silver tiara added the crowning touch. She had felt like a true princess, and everything was perfect...until after the ball.

Miss Craig decided the prince and princess should be formally presented to the student body during the weekly assembly program. Prince Timothy had a beautiful voice, and her plan was to have the royal couple sing a duet. Annie recalled Miss Craig's very words: "I will select a simple song that anyone can sing." Anyone did not include Annie. Miss Craig chose another song, and another, and another. Annie could not sing any of them well enough for a duet. As a last resort, she and the prince stood on the stage in their royal finery and led the students in singing "God Bless America." Timothy did a great job.

After other disappointments, Annie finally accepted the fact that she could not sing. She reluctantly became a dancing bear or a butterfly, or helped with the scenery, or made the announcements. Something always was found for Annie to do that did not involve singing.

Finishing first among the thirteen members of her eighth grade class, Annie looked forward to attending high school. There she learned, however, that she would be required to participate in either the band or the chorus. She felt sure she could never learn to play an instrument so she opted for chorus, feeling she could bluff her way by pretending to sing. She soon found that Miss Gunter, the chorus director, had plans that did not include bluffers. "Everyone can sing. Every person has a singing voice," Miss Gunter said, "but it may take some work to find it." During the first few weeks she taught the students to stand correctly and breathe deeply, to "float" the high notes, to enunciate correctly, not "squeeze" the vowels, and blend together in a single voice. Annie was an eager learner. For the first time in her life, there was someone who believed she could sing. As she worked under Miss Gunter's direction, her voice developed and she gained confidence, practicing long hours to reach her potential. Annie's proudest moment came in her senior year, when she sang a solo in the chorus' final performance.

Now it was payback time. As the children entered the music room, Annie looked into their faces and smiled. She recognized these little ones as potential soloists, knowing that the ability to sing is not limited to a few special persons. It is a God–given gift to all of His children, but it's a gift some must work diligently to find. It would be not only her responsibility, but also her joy, to lead in that search. She wanted to instill in the heart, soul, and mind of every child the truth she herself had learned from a dedicated teacher—a teacher who had opened a whole new world for her with the simple but profound statement, "Everyone can sing."

A GIFT FROM GOD

Hear now this story
About two people in love
And how they are blessed
By the Father above.

Bobby asked of Patia,
"Will you marry me?"
Thus the two became one
And soon will be three.

The happiness they've found
Has but only begun;
Through love that they share
God is sending a son.

A bundle from Heaven
Who right from the start
With a twitch of a smile
Will melt every heart.

With ten little fingers
Ten wee, tiny toes,
A rosebud–like mouth,
A button of a nose.

Though helpless and small,
What a miracle he'll be,
For a bit of each parent
In his life we will see.

Tending to son's needs
Will require much attention;
He will add to their lives
A whole new dimension.

As parents they'll find
With the son they adore,
There will come some nights
They'll be walking the floor.

For parenthood is not easy;
Things don't always go nice.
Though heartaches may come,
It's well worth the price.

So, to Patia and Bobby,
And the baby God's sending,
May your blessings be many,
And your joy never ending.

Written in honor of Patia and Bobby Johnson
as they awaited the birth of their first child.

WITHOUT EYES TO SEE

Jimmy was blind. His dark glasses concealed eyes that once saw the beauty of God's creation, but now could detect little more than mere shadows. He carried a white cane as he crossed the busy streets of downtown Memphis, hurrying to the building where he operated a lobby concession stand.

After an introduction, Jimmy seemed to recognize every person's voice. He called his regular customers by name when responding to their greetings. His cheerfulness made it easy to forget that he could not see.

One day I was talking with him about two brothers who shared an office in the building. At that time I had met only one of the men, but Jimmy apparently knew both. He spoke with such familiarity that before I thought, I asked if the brothers looked alike. Realizing what I had asked, I stammered with embarrassment. Jimmy laughed as he told me that one of the men was taller than the other. This he had "seen" with his ears.

Some of us use our handicaps as crutches. Not Jimmy. He never considered himself to be blind—only that he had no eyesight.

I am thankful that our paths crossed and I am grateful to Jimmy for the lessons I learned from him. His vision excelled that of many who are blessed with perfect eyesight, for he walked with one hand clasping a white cane and the other holding fast to the hand of God.

JIMMY'S EASTER SURPRISE

Easter was one of Jimmy's favorite holidays. Maybe it wasn't as exciting as Christmas, but there were a lot of things that made Easter very special.

Jimmy liked the Easter story. It was in his book of Bible stories that his dad read to him when he was little. Now that he was in the second grade, he could read it by himself, except for a few big words. But he still liked for his dad and mother to read to him.

Being eight years old, he understood the real meaning of Easter. He knew that on that first Easter morning, Jesus had come alive again and had come right out of his grave, which really was like a big cave. And the big, big stone that had blocked the entrance to the cave had been rolled away. He liked to think about how excited Jesus's friends were when the angel told them He was alive again. Sometimes he thought about what he would have done if he had been there. He would have run as fast as he could to tell everybody what had happened.

Jimmy was looking forward to going to Sunday School and church on Easter morning. He knew there would be Easter lilies on the altar rail, all across the front of the church, and everyone would be dressed especially nice.

Jimmy's mother had taken him shopping. He had a new blue suit and a white shirt, and a tie just like his dad's. He knew that people wear their "good clothes" to church on Sunday because going to God's house is special. And Easter Sunday is even more special. He would be wearing some brand new clothes, and so would most of his friends, as a way to celebrate the new life that Jesus had when he came alive again.

Jimmy went to a big church, with beautiful stained glass windows. His church had both a piano and an organ. He liked the music. On Easter there probably would be special music on the chimes and bells, and maybe even trumpets. And, at the end of the service, the choir would sing the "Hallelujah Chorus." That was the most exciting part.

On Saturday, the day before Easter, there would be an egg hunt at the church for all the children. Afterwards they would go into the fellowship hall for cookies and pink lemonade. Those who had found a lot of eggs would divide with those who didn't find many. He usually would find enough to fill his basket. He was a good egg–hunter, and he didn't mind sharing with the other boys and girls. He really liked to hunt eggs, and he had his basket ready.

On Good Friday, the day before the egg hunt, there was a phone call from Jimmy's grandmother. Grandpa had fallen and broken his arm. They really wanted Dad and Mother and Jimmy to come for the weekend. Of course, Dad said they would leave early the next morning.

Jimmy's grandparents lived on a farm about two hundred miles away. He liked to visit them, and he was very sorry about Grandpa's broken arm. But now he was going to miss going to Sunday School and to his own church on Easter Sunday. And he would miss the egg hunt, too.

He knew they would go to church on Easter, but his grandparents' church was nothing like his. It was just a little white church, not brick like his. It didn't have pretty stained glass windows or an organ. They had a piano and just a few people in their choir. He figured they didn't even know the "Hallelujah Chorus." They probably wouldn't even have any Easter lilies.

Jimmy was in for a lot of surprises.

First of all, there were Easter lilies—a lot of them—on the piano and all around the pulpit.

But what Jimmy noticed first was a big wooden cross, not a pretty one. Just two rough boards nailed together to make a cross and there was some kind of wire over it. It looked like the kind of wire Grandpa had around his chicken pen. It had little holes in it. He wondered why the church had such an ugly cross.

After the preacher had welcomed everybody and they had prayed, the preacher said they were going to "flower the cross." Jimmy wondered what that meant.

Then some of the ladies came in with all kinds of flowers. There were buttercups and lilies and flowers of all colors. Everyone was given a flower to put onto the cross. Jimmy knew now why it was covered with wire with the little holes because the flowers were stuck through the holes. The tallest people put their flowers up high where the little ones couldn't reach. When all the flowers had been put on, the ugly cross had turned into the most beautiful cross Jimmy had ever seen.

The choir did know the "Hallelujah Chorus" and the whole church was invited to become "auxiliary choir members" and join the choir on the final chorus.

Grandma and Grandpa's church was a lot different from Jimmy's, but the Easter story was the same!

After dinner Dad said it was time to start back home. It had been a good Easter. Jimmy hadn't missed anything really...except the egg hunt.

But Grandma had a surprise. "Wait," she said, "Jimmy hasn't had his egg hunt." She took him by his hand and off they went to the chicken house.

Along the walls of the chicken house were rows of boxes and in each box there was a nest made of straw. These were where the chickens laid their eggs.

"Come, Jimmy," said Grandma, "and look into this first box."

At first Jimmy couldn't see anything except a big fat hen sitting on a nest. As he looked closer, he could see some eggs in the nest. Then he heard a little cracking sound and a tiny little peep. Then another and another. Right before his eyes, the eggs were beginning to crack open and out were coming teeny, tiny, little baby chickens!

Jimmy had never seen anything like that before!

The baby chicks were coming out of the eggs on Easter Sunday, just like Jesus had come out of His grave.

Jimmy did just what he knew he would have done on that very first Easter. He turned and ran to tell the good news.

"Come and see! Come and see!" he shouted. "God has sent another Easter miracle...right in Grandpa's chicken house!"

REMEMBER MUNICH

It was our wedding anniversary. We had just finished a wonderful dinner at one of our favorite restaurants and were enjoying one last cup of coffee as we waited for the server to bring our check. "I'm going to the ladies' room," I said to my husband Felix, "and if I'm not back in five minutes..."

"I know," he said with a smile and an affirmative nod of his head, "I should come looking for you."

I wondered if he really would check on me or would he just keep waiting, like he had done that morning in Munich. Although it happened more than a dozen years earlier, the incident was as vivid in my mind as though it were yesterday.

We had gone to Germany on a combined business and pleasure trip. Having packed boots and heavy coats, we thought we were prepared for a cold but pleasant winter vacation. The snowstorm was totally unexpected.

The huge flakes began falling the day we arrived and continued all week. The news media confirmed what we heard local people saying everywhere we went: "Munich Hit by Heaviest Snowstorm in 10 Years." Many streets were impassable, schools were closed, and parks were filled with children on sleds.

Our first venture outside of the hotel was to buy fur–lined hats with flaps to cover our ears. Dressed warmly with flexible plans, we found the snow exciting and only slightly inconvenient. Although taxis were practically non–existent, our hotel was within walking distance of the train station. As we trampled along toward the station early one morning to board a train to Austria, we could hardly see for the swirling snow. A small sidewalk café seemed to be beckoning us to stop for coffee.

"No more than twenty minutes," Felix warned, "or we'll miss our train."

Although the manager spoke little English and our German vocabulary was very limited, we settled into a booth and soon were enjoying cups of steaming black coffee. Two things were noticed immediately—the café offered strong, but delicious coffee and provided very loud music! The coffee was to our liking. The music would have hastened us on our way even if we were not in somewhat of a hurry to catch our train.

Draining the last drop from my cup, I said to Felix, "I'm going to make a quick trip to the ladies' room; I'm leaving my purse with you." I hurried down the dimly lighted steps at the rear of the café to the basement where the restrooms were located.

International symbols are wonderful, removing any doubt as to which was for women. The door to the stall I entered closed with a bang. Seconds later I realized I was locked inside. There was no hardware on the inside of the stall door and, since I had left my purse with Felix, I didn't even have a fingernail file that I might have somehow used to force the lock. Moreover, there was no "crawl space" at the bottom of the door and only about twelve inches between the top of the door and the ceiling. I was in deep trouble!

I screamed for help, thinking Felix would come running to my rescue, but soon realized he probably could not hear me above the loud music. It crossed my mind, too, if he heard my frantic cries, he likely would be in such a panic that he might leave my purse with our traveler's checks and passports. As I pondered my predicament, I heard water running in the adjoining men's room. I felt better, knowing I had only to listen for the water to stop and for the sound of the door opening and closing. Then I would start screaming again, and whoever was there would surely come in and rescue me.

Shortly I heard the footsteps of someone leaving the men's room and I began screaming for help, banging my fists against the stall door. I stood on the bottom hinge and peeped through the small opening above the door. It seemed an eternity before I saw the restroom door begin to open very slowly. Cautiously peering inside was a tall man in an army–type trench coat. His bearded face and long matted hair gave evidence to his being a "street person," who probably had been using the men's restroom for his limited bathing. From the bewildered look on his face, I knew he did not understand English. In another situation, I would have wanted to distance myself from him. Now I was hanging onto the top of the door with one hand and waving the other one through the opening, motioning for him to come inside and free me from my entrapment. Looking around like a scared rabbit, he finally stepped inside and with a turn of the handle, opened the stall door.

I ran out of the restroom and up the steps with my rescuer in pursuit, giving me rear–end pats as I tried to escape him. Falling into the arms of Felix, I tried to explain the horrible ordeal. The commotion got the attention of the manager. He quickly escorted the man out of the café, although he never understood what I was trying to tell him about the lock on the stall door.

Now I enter public restrooms with a whole new prospective. I check the lock and hardware before closing the stall door, and I feel extra smug if there is "crawl space" below. When I'm with my husband I always remind him to check on me if I'm not back in five minutes. I know I'm paranoid about this, but it's a serious matter. Forever and a day, I will remember Munich.

MY HUSBAND, THE NEAT FREAK

My husband Norman and I are living proof that opposites attract. He is a dyed–in–the–wool neat freak. I am having a good day if my socks match.

I spotted Norman when he walked into the room where men and women I didn't recognize were gathering for our 35th high school reunion. He wore a blue–and–white striped shirt that was void of the slightest wrinkle. His trousers were perfectly creased and his shoes looked as if they had been given more attention than I had spent on my entire weekend wardrobe. He was totally neat, and he was single!

Norman was no longer the skinny boy with red hair and freckles that I vaguely remembered from our ninth–grade math class. His hair had darkened over the years, the freckles had somewhat faded, and his slender six–foot frame gave credibility to the rumor that he could be found most weekdays on the golf course. I liked what I saw. Before the evening was over he had accepted my dinner invitation, albeit with a bit of hesitation. I don't know why men are so suspicious of such innocent acts of kindness.

My qualifications as a contender for this prize specimen were limited, but I had a few things in my favor. I had been widowed twelve years earlier when my three children were teenagers. Now they were all out of the nest and urging their mother to feather it again. Added to this was my expertise in the kitchen. I knew the way to a man's heart was through his stomach and I was planning a direct cardiac route before Mr. Neatnik ever had a hunger pain.

The first real clue I had as to Norman's total commitment to neatness came when he arrived at my house for dinner. If he had come directly from the dealer's showroom, his car could not have looked better. No dents. No bents. No smudges. No bugs on the windshield. No bird had dared to fly over his car.

I had an uneasy feeling that I may have been a little hasty with the dinner invitation. Norman probably didn't allow dust balls under his furniture, but surely he would understand that I couldn't throw out last week's newspapers until I had time to read the obituaries. It was just that removing the month's accumulation from the kitchen counters, and putting away the laundry that I didn't finish over the weekend because of the reunion, had taken more time than I had anticipated. I did regret, however, that the costumes my grandchildren had worn two weeks earlier in the Fourth of July parade were still piled on the end of the living room sofa.

But love is blind, and this wonderful man did not seem to notice that I tend to be somewhat less than neat. I felt confident that in time I could help him overcome this obsession for neatness and we would be able to strike a happy medium. It was a leap year and I leapt. Four months later we were married.

We began our life together in the house where I had lived for fifteen years. I had not realized so many improvements were needed. For the next three years Norman had little time for golf. First he tackled the garage. He built work benches and installed shelving and peg boards. There was no way he could begin a project without adequate space to work and easy accessibility to his tools. Next came the renovation of our bedroom closet. He installed new rods for hanging shorter garments above the existing rods, shelves for hats and such, and racks for all our shoes.

The finished product was remarkable. Our closet space was doubled. But try as I might, I couldn't keep my side as tidy as his. It was difficult to keep my shoes lined up orderly on the little shelves when I was in the habit of opening the closet door and kicking them inside. Norman never complained. When the floor was so littered with my shoes that the door wouldn't close, he would pick them up and put them neatly on the racks.

Finally I was getting accustomed to all the new shelves and cabinets and learning where I could hide half–eaten candy bars when we decided to buy another house. Norman had to start over again. First the garage and workshop. Then the closets with extra rods and rows of shoe racks. We closed on an early afternoon and by that evening everything was in its proper place. Dishes were in the cabinets, books on the shelves. Even our pictures were hung at the carefully measured height and most suitable wall position.

Within three months Norman had painted the outside of the house. The original color did not blend with the shingles on the roof.

Our lawn soon looked better than the greens at the golf course, which Norman saw less of now than when he was single. He fertilized, watered, trimmed, edged and mowed. If a weed dared to show its ugly head, its days were numbered. We had the showplace of the neighborhood for three years. Then we moved again.

It's hard to believe we have been in our present home more than six years. Last summer Norman replaced the back deck. I was his apprentice. I had two major responsibilities. I pulled all the nails out of the old boards as he pried them up, just to lessen the possibility of anyone stepping on a nail before the boards could be disposed of. My other job was to hold a spacer between the boards as each was screwed to the foundation to assure that the space between every board was exactly the same. There are no nails in our new deck. Only screws, all in perfect lines. Of course Norman personally selected every piece of lumber to be sure it wasn't warped or didn't have excessive knotholes.

The winter months are the worst for Norman. He is running out of inside things that need his neat touch. He has made new shelves in the utility room so the soft drinks can be properly stored and not left on the floor where I have always put them. He built book shelves, floor to ceiling, across one end of our living room. The walk–in closet in our bedroom could be featured in "Home Beautiful" if my side were not always in disarray.

Last week when I was putting away the laundry, I opened Norman's sock drawer and saw that my neat freak had been at it again. His cold–weather socks were neatly stacked, by colors, in the front of the drawer and the ones he wears during the summer months had been moved to the back. His underwear drawer was equally as neat—V-neck undershirts in one stack, round–neck undershirts in another, shorts neatly folded and stacked in one corner. Not wanting to inadvertently put his socks or underwear in the wrong stack, I left his things on the bed. Better for him to put them away than me since I don't have much experience with folding and stacking.

To be sure, there are many advantages to having a neatnik husband. Norman has taken over a lot of the household chores. I praise him for how well he vacuums the carpet and dusts the furniture, and I assure him that he irons much better than I. My fear is that this may be coming to an end. He no longer has his summer shirts on white hangers, fall clothes on yellow hangers, winter jackets and coats on red, and his spring wardrobe on green.

I really hate to see him change. I love him just the way he is. After all, it was his neatness that first attracted me. But either he is mellowing with age or finally has decided it's more fun on the golf course than in the broom closet.

THE GHOST AND
MR. MAGUIRE

It was just as well no one bothered to inform John Maguire or his wife Mary that the house they were buying was haunted. Anyone with the knowledge and sophistication of Attorney John Jason Maguire would know that ghosts are figments of one's imagination.

The house was exactly what they wanted. They knew the moment they drove past. That is, when they almost drove past. John had slammed on the brakes as they rounded the corner and saw the big "FOR SALE" sign in the front yard. Had they not taken the wrong turn out of the airport (Mary's fault, of course) and then had to detour for road repair, they might never have seen the grand old mansion. Mary was certain it was fate, not coincidence, that had put them there.

Painted white, the two–story house sat a distance from the street in a thick grove of trees. A wide porch wrapped around the front and sides. The double front doors opened into a 12–foot–wide hallway, with a rear stairway leading to the second floor. The rooms, with beautiful oak floors and 14–foot ceilings, were awesome. There was even a large attic room that would be a perfect studio for Mary's painting and sculpturing.

The real estate agent said the house had just been put on the market, although it had been vacant for some time while the heirs emptied it of the furnishings and made minor repairs. In actuality, the house had been listed with the Realtor for more than three years, and he was excited to have found prospective buyers, for it was talked around town that the old house was haunted.

It was a much bigger house than they needed, now that the older daughters were married and there were only the two of them and eight–year–old Meghan; however, both John and Mary were drawn to the house in a strange, almost magical, way. They moved in the last day of August, just in time to get settled before the start of Meghan's school.

John's law office was a twenty–minute drive from the house, which allowed him sometimes to have lunch at home with his wife. More often than not, however, Mary would be at a meeting of the garden club, the book club, or participating in some local civic activity. She was the perfect suburban housewife.

Within a few weeks an early frost turned the leaves on the trees to bright yellow and orange. They marveled at the beauty that surrounded them, feeling they were blessed beyond measure to have found such a perfect home.

Most evenings John could be found sitting before the open fire in the family room. He read journals or reviewed case histories while Meghan did homework. Mary often joined them, sometimes knitting, but more often writing to their older daughters about their new home and the enjoyment of suburban living. It was on such an evening in late October that Meghan asked her father who was the man she had seen standing by the fireplace when she came in from school that afternoon.

The apple of her father's eye, Meghan seldom did or said anything that displeased John. When much younger, she had amused her parents as she related incidents involving her imaginary friends. Now a reprimand was in order, for John felt his daughter should have outgrown her childish tales.

"A man in our house! Impossible!" he admonished.

Nothing John said would make Meghan admit that this was one of her made–up stories. She described in detail the man she has seen, saying that he was not much taller than she and was very thin. She remembered that he was wearing blue overalls and a funny little hat. He was holding something in his left hand that looked like a small tool box. After hanging her coat in the closet, she had turned and he was gone.

Deciding it was best to say nothing more and hope Meghan would soon forget the whole episode, John kissed his daughter goodnight.

Several nights later, as John sat alone by the fireplace reading and enjoying the warmth of the fading embers, he was startled to hear a distinct creaking noise. It was as though someone were slowly coming down the stairs. Mary and Meghan had gone to bed quite early, and he felt certain both were asleep. Quickly he arose and tiptoed across the room. Peeping through the doorway, his eyes traveled up and down the stairs. He saw no one. Reasoning that it was only the wind, he returned to his chair; however the book no longer held his interest. Although he had locked the doors earlier, he checked them once again before retiring.

A few nights later, alone in the house, John again heard footsteps on the stairs. As before, he saw no one. Was someone hiding in the attic, coming down at night?

Who was this person and how was he, or she, able to disappear so quickly?

John was an intelligent, highly regarded attorney. His motto was "often wrong but never in doubt." Now he was beginning to have serious doubts about his own sanity. Evidently neither Mary nor Meghan had heard the footsteps, and he decided it best not to mention this to anyone, especially not to Mary. She likely would want him to see a psychiatrist. Possibly she would have him committed to a mental institution. No, he decided, he would not share this with anyone.

Over the next few weeks John continued to hear footsteps late at night. Other than that, he did not see or hear anything that seemed out of the ordinary.

December brought freezing temperatures and frozen pipes. A plumber was called to replace pipes that had burst with the thaw. He was a personable young man, working quickly and efficiently. John invited him to have a cup of coffee before he left. As they sat at the kitchen table, the man commented that he had been in the house many times before old Mr. McElmee, the former owner, died. Mr. McElmee had been his mentor and had taught him everything he knew about plumbing.

John listened intently. He suddenly felt as if there were someone else in the room with them. He couldn't shake the eerie feeling that had come over him and he wanted to hear more about the former owner of the house.

"Well," said the young man, "he was a friendly old gentleman. Never met a stranger. He was born here in this house, lived here all his life, and died right there in the front room. He wasn't what one would call good looking. Hardly five feet tall and quite thin. He never married and during the last years of his life, he became somewhat of a hermit. He didn't leave this house often after he quit plumbing. He even had his groceries delivered from the corner store."

A chill ran down John's spine as the young man laughed and said, "What I remember most about him, though, from earlier years when he still did plumbing work around town, were the overalls and that funny little hat he always wore. And no matter where he went, he always took his tool box."

John paid the plumber, surprising him with a very generous tip. After all, now he knew he wasn't losing his mind. In fact, it was rather comforting to know old Mr. McElmee was still keeping an eye on things.

THE RING

Tears streamed down Anna's face as she looked with disbelief at the pinkie finger of her right hand. Gone was the tiny gold ring with the square–cut ruby, bearing the insignia of the prestigious fraternal organization. The ring had been her dearest treasure for many years, and its loss had cast a veil of gloom over the forthcoming Christmas holidays.

Anna's mother had worn the ring, along with her gold wedding band, until the day of her death. A generation earlier it had belonged to Anna's grandmother. But it was her Great Grandmother Jessie for whom the ring had been specially designed and handcrafted. Anna knew the story well, for she had heard it many times.

Great Grandmother Jessie's father, William John Weir, and several others of her kin, had been members of a mysterious fraternal order to which no female ever had been admitted. Anna knew that for more than four generations the organization had not deviated from its rule that barred women from its membership—with one exception.

As a child, Jessie had been curious about the organization. Her father had a small black leather book, which he kept locked in his chest. He always took the book with him to the monthly meetings and replaced it in the chest when he returned. Even if the chest had not been locked, she would not have dared to explore the contents of the book. Respect for one's property was strictly adhered to among members of her family.

Jessie was eleven years of age when she had an opportunity to satisfy her curiosity. A meeting of the brotherhood was to be held in their home. Long before the first member arrived, she had found a hiding place behind the folds of the heavy curtains in the room where the men would gather. Thinking that Jessie had gone with her sister to visit a neighbor, no one gave thought as to her whereabouts. Safely out of sight, she listened intently as the meeting was called to order and the men recited the motto and purpose in unison. She liked the part about giving assistance to widows and orphans and providing financial aid to underprivileged students. It soon became apparent to her that the main item of business was application for membership from several men in the community. Jessie strained to listen to every word as the men discussed each applicant. She found some of the information to be totally shocking, especially that which she heard about two of the deacons in the church she and her family regularly attended.

Everything would have gone perfectly had she not sneezed. Never had Jessie seen her father so angry. The men decided there was only one thing to do since she had been privy to everything that had transpired. They would have to accept her into the brotherhood, having her swear on her honor never to reveal what she had overheard. To remind her of the oath she had taken, the special ring was designed and given to her.

Upon Jessie's death, the ring was left to her daughter, then to Anna's mother, and eventually it was bequeathed to Anna. Now the precious ring was gone.

Anna recalled that she had worn the ring two days earlier when she went to the neighborhood garden center to purchase Christmas poinsettias. She always bought six. One she would place on the altar rail at her church in memory of her mother. Two were for the secretaries in her husband's office, and three for the nursing home where her mother had spent the last few months of her life. She couldn't remember why she wore the ring that day. She didn't wear it often. Maybe it was because she was thinking of her mother and was in a melancholy mood that she took the ring from her jewelry case and slipped it onto her finger.

The poinsettias seemed especially beautiful that year and Anna had spent nearly an hour choosing the ones she would buy. She had taken them to her home and had placed three on either side of the fireplace, with the intent of keeping them a few days before making the deliveries. She was seated on the sofa, admiring their beauty and enjoying a cup of coffee, when she realized the ring was missing from her finger.

The classified ad, with offer of a sizeable reward, had brought no response, nor had the posters she had tacked to the bulletin board at the garden center. She had searched every inch of her car and carefully gone through the contents of her purse and pockets. The ring had once fit tightly, but because of her recent weight loss, it had been a bit loose on her finger. But she never thought it would slip off.

Holiday parties and preparing for church programs kept Anna busy during the week before Christmas. She baked cookies for her husband's office party and delivered the poinsettias to the secretaries. She spent half a day at the nursing home, exchanging hugs with the residents who thanked her for brightening their holidays with the beautiful plants. She had taken one of the poinsettias to her church a week before Christmas, placing it on the altar rail with dozens of others that beautified the sanctuary. Although she participated in all the usual activities, the missing ring was never far from her thoughts. It was hard to accept the fact that it was gone forever.

As was their custom, Anna and her family attended a candlelight service at their church on Christmas Eve. From her seat in the third pew, she noticed right away that the poinsettia she had placed on the altar stood out from all the rest—not because it was more beautiful, but because its leaves were beginning to curl. While the others looked fresh and colorful, hers was beginning to droop, as if begging for attention—perhaps needing water. She had not properly cared for the poinsettias she had bought that year. They were only a reminder of her great loss. Had she not gone to the garden center to buy them, the ring might still be in her jewelry case.

As members of the congregation left the church at the close of the service, Anna walked to the altar and reached for the poinsettia she had brought. She pushed aside the leaves to see if the plant was dry. As she pressed her fingers onto the soil, she felt something that sent a chill down her spine. Dropping to her knees, she pushed back the red foil covering the pot and raised the lower leaves of the poinsettia. There it was—the ring she had never expected to see again! Was it only by chance that her ring had fallen into this plant—the one she had placed on the altar in her mother's memory? Was it merely a coincidence that she had decided to check the moisture of the soil before she left the sanctuary that night? Definitely not! As the altar candles cast their glow on the upheld ring, Anna knew this was her very own Christmas miracle.

PITCHING A HISSY FIT

"Don't pitch a hissy fit!" I probably heard Mama say that to me a thousand times before I was half grown. "Now, Sara Jane," she'd say, "you are a lady and don't you ever forget it."

I hate to admit it, but I forgot Mama's words the day before Thanksgiving, and I pitched a good one. Or I reckon Mama would call it a hissy fit. I've never known exactly what one of those is because it's not in my dictionary. I'm sure, though, it is when one says or does something unladylike. That being the case, I sure pitched one.

Although I live alone now, I wanted to have a traditional Thanksgiving dinner. I knew I wouldn't have time to cook a turkey since I had to work all day on Wednesday, so I stopped at the delicatessen that morning on the way to the office and placed an order for a five–pound turkey breast, three pounds of cornbread dressing and a pint of giblet gravy. I was assured it would be ready when I stopped that afternoon on my way home from work. On my limited budget, I couldn't afford to have the deli prepare the vegetables and dessert, but I could do that Thanksgiving morning, and also make a cranberry salad.

Evidently there were a lot of other people who had placed orders at the delicatessen because the pick–up line was as long as the one at the ladies' room at half-time during the ball games. I took a number and by the time it was called, my feet were aching and my spirits had sunk to a new low. The worse was yet to come. The employee could not find my order. That was when I pitched the hissy fit and demanded to see the manager on duty. That poor soul may never have seen a hissy fit being pitched, but he got the full load. It didn't take him long to find my order—however it had not been prepared. He apologized profusely and promised to have it ready at 9:00 o'clock the next morning, Thanksgiving Day…with his compliments. That calmed me down considerably.

The employee who had been the first recipient of my wrath the previous evening was back on the job Thanksgiving morning when I went by to pick up the order. Needless to say, she recognized me instantly and apologized again for my inconvenience as she handed me the large take–out box. She was so nice, I felt a little remorseful for having pitched the hissy fit. I muttered a weak thank–you and made a hasty exit to my car. When I opened the box at home, I felt even more ashamed. My order had been doubled, courtesy of the delicatessen. Two five–pound turkey breasts, six pounds of dressing and a full quart of giblet gravy, with a personal note from the manager apologizing again and wishing me a happy Thanksgiving. I could almost see Mama shaking her head at me in disgust.

Before I had finished unpacking the box, the phone rang. A distress call from my young next–door neighbor. Her husband's parents and several of his other relatives had been invited for dinner. Her turkey had turned out dry and tasteless. "No problem," I said, "just meet me at the fence." She burst into tears when I presented her with a five–pound turkey breast, ready to serve, along with dressing and gravy.

"Well, Mama," I thought as I was enjoying my free Thanksgiving dinner, "pitching that hissy fit wasn't so bad after all…but I will try to behave better."

My good intentions didn't last long. Less than a week later I pitched another one! I had stopped by the "fast–fish" place for a nine–piece takeout order of batter–dipped, greasy fried, cholesterol–loaded fish filets with a double order of french fries. My cousin from up North was visiting and I wanted him to enjoy some Southern delicacies. I grabbed a $10 dollar bill out of my wallet and hurried inside, leaving my purse in the car. I knew the order, with my senior discount, should be just a little more than nine dollars. When the young lady entered my order into the computer, she informed me the total was $10.16. Of course I knew right off what was wrong. "You didn't give me my senior discount," I explained, confidant that I had requested it when I ordered. Without hesitating, she said I wasn't entitled to a discount. It is definitely obvious from my gray hair and wrinkled skin that I qualify for Medicare and any other benefits available to those of us in our golden years. I waited for an explanation.

"We only give the discount when you order the two–piece dinner or the one-piece special."

I argued that I was spending more than twice what one of the regular dinners would cost and it was totally ridiculous that I could not get the senior discount. I insisted that she check with the manager on duty. She left and I felt confident that she would be reprimanded for her stupidity. Waiting impatiently, I noticed that the line of customers behind me had lengthened considerably. I was sorry to inconvenience them, but being a senior citizen has very few advantages, and I was determined to get what was due me.

Although I had created a slight disturbance earlier, it wasn't until the young lady finally came back from checking with the manager that I threw my hissy fit. She was downright snippy when she informed me that she was right. I definitely could not have a senior discount. I shook my head in disbelief. "Well," I said, "You will just have to wait until I go out to the car and get your sixteen cents." When I came back, the man who had been in the line behind me grinned and said, "You can keep your money, lady, I paid the sixteen cents for you." I tried to repay him, but he was determined not to accept my money. Moreover, he said the three quarters on the counter beside my sacked order were also mine.

"No, they aren't," I insisted.

"Yes, they are," he said. The other customers watched and listened in obvious amusement as we continued to argue over the seventy–five cents that the man explained would make up for the senior discount, which he agreed I rightfully deserved.

Since it was the principle of the matter and not the money itself, there was no way I would accept the three quarters. I picked up my fish and fries and headed for the door. It was that sassy young lady behind the counter who had the last word. As I was leaving, I heard her say, "If nobody else wants this money, I'll take it myself."

I know Mama would not approve of my outbursts, but there are times when the situation calls for desperate measures, and the only appropriate action is a genuine "hissy fit!"

ABOUT THE AUTHOR...

*A*nne Hall Norris, the youngest of eight children, is a native of Memphis, Tenn., and has never lived more than a few miles from her place of birth. At age eighteen, she married Jack Wagoner. Their three children were teenagers when he suffered a fatal heart attack. Twelve years later at a high school reunion she renewed acquaintance with former classmate Felix Norris. They celebrated their 17th wedding anniversary in the year 2000. Her love for writing was nurtured in high school, where she was associate editor of the school paper. Later as a young mother, she edited a countywide weekly newspaper, followed by a 32–year career with the International Association of Holiday Inns, Inc. Extensive travel with the hotel system took her to more than 30 foreign countries. Since her retirement, she and her husband continue to travel and have toured the entire United States. She is a former member of the Ninety–Nines, Inc., an international organization of licensed women pilots founded by Amelia Earhart, and participated several years in the Powder Puff Derby, the all–woman transcontinental air race. A member of the Story Tellers' League of Memphis since 1992, she was elected president of the organization in 2000 and devotes countless hours *sharing stories with schools, nursing and retirement homes, and various other groups throughout the Memphis area. She and her husband are members of Oakhaven United Methodist Church, where she teaches Sunday School, is a member of the choir, serves on the administrative board and the council on ministries and is active in the United Methodist Women. She credits her family, including four granddaughters and her brother Frank, with providing ideas and inspiration for many of the stories included in this book.*

ABOUT THE ARTIST...

Gary Wagoner, who provided the illustrations for this book, is the elder son of the author and her late husband Jack Wagoner. He resides in Germantown, Tenn., with his wife Beverly and their teenage daughters, Allison and Jennifer. A graduate of Auburn University, he is a licensed architect and vice-president of Construction Management Plus, Inc. His hobbies include disc golf and sailing. He is proficient on guitar, banjo and several other musical instruments and often entertains his friends and family.